I0762534

Friends of the Good

Friends of the Good

How Remarkable Friendships Transform Our Lives

Demond Martin

with Corey Hajim

NEW YORK

STOREHOUSE VOICES
An imprint of the Crown Publishing Group
A division of Penguin Random House LLC
1745 Broadway
New York, NY 10019
storehousevoices.com
penguinrandomhouse.com

Background image on title page spread: Shutterstock.com/fotoak

Library of Congress Cataloging-in-Publication Data has been applied for.

ISBN 979-8-21708-758-7
Ebook ISBN 979-8-21708-759-4

Editor: Jennifer Baker
Production editor: Christine Tanigawa
Text designer: Andrea Lau
Production: Heather Williamson
Copy editor: Maureen Clark
Proofreaders: Lisa Lawley, Katie Powers

Manufactured in the United States of America

1st Printing

First Edition

The authorized representative in the EU for product safety and compliance is Penguin Random House Ireland, Morrison Chambers, 32 Nassau Street, Dublin D02 YH68, Ireland, https://eu-contact.penguin.ie.

For Kia, Teddy, and Jordan

Your love is my foundation.
Your joy is my purpose.

CONTENTS

FOREWORD

As iron sharpens iron, so a friend sharpens a friend.

—PROVERBS 27:17

Sometime over the past decade the word *friend* became a verb. It was attached not so much to the nomenclature of nurturing meaningful relationships as to the act of clicking an icon on some kind of device to signal a thumbs-up in a social media space. "Friending" someone through the push of a few buttons is quick and easy and momentarily satisfying, though never quite as edifying as the act of actually befriending someone because that requires something more tangible.

To befriend someone means that you are present in the life of another human being, even if you are separated by distance. It quite literally means being there for someone, whether in proximity, on the phone, or just by providing the supreme gift of knowing there is a person in this vast universe who understands your heart, celebrates your quirks, tolerates your moods (and your weird musical choices), keeps it real—and tells you like it is—protects your interests, laughs at your bad jokes, invests in your well-being, and genuinely wants you to always, and in all ways, find your best self.

Friendship is one of life's greatest gifts and yet we so often take it for granted, especially in adulthood when we get busy and bogged down with life's responsibilities. Right around the time that new technologies were creating ways for us to "friend" each other in the virtual world, America slid into something sociologists called a "Friendship Recession"[1] in the real world. Surveys were showing that more people were claiming to have fewer close friends. About one-third of Americans claimed to have ten or more close friends in 1990.[2] By 2020, that number had decreased to just over 12 percent, and that drop was most pronounced for men.

This deficit has consequences. Former U.S. Surgeon General Vivek Murthy issued a warning about an epidemic of loneliness in 2023 and noted it as a public health crisis.[3] He cited studies showing loneliness is linked to an increased risk for heart disease, stroke, stomach ailments, and even dementia. Loneliness and social isolation have the same negative health impact as smoking fifteen cigarettes a day.

One of the key antidotes to this growing deficit is figuring out how to create pathways for meaningful interaction. But what exactly does that mean? And what are the implications for men, who are more likely to view the emotional depth of highly participatory, fully interactive friendship as something that seems more naturally instinctive for women? Let's face it, women are more likely to bring an enthusiastic, high-octane, let-me-show-ya-how-it's-done energy to organizing a girls' trip, game night, potluck, Bible study, book club, color-coordinated sit-and-sip, or meal delivery for a sick neighbor.

It's not that women are better at friendships. Their rules of engagement are often different. I had long been aware of this so-called friendship deficit in America, but a segment with Jane Fonda on *CBS News Sunday Morning* really drove home the point for me. She was being interviewed along with costars Lily Tomlin, Sally Field, and Rita Moreno about their Super Bowl chick flick *80 for Brady*. All of them were looking fabulous, and though you knew they were required to be there to promote a feel-good film, you got the sense that there was a genuine circle of admiration among these Silver Queens, who had probably all been pitted against one another at one time or another in the cutthroat world of Hollywood. It was clear they admired and respected each other—even when the cameras stopped rolling.

Jane Fonda noted that her "favorite ex-husband, who's Ted Turner," had at one point pronounced that no one makes real friends after the age of sixty. She thought he was wrong, but she conceded that climbing the hill toward meaningful friendship was less steep for women.

"Women's friendships are very different than men's friendships, and they're very important to our health," Fonda said to a male interviewer who seemed not exactly skeptical but also not fully convinced.

She pressed on, explaining, "You guys, you kind of sit side by side and watch sports or cars or women. Women sit facing each other, eye to eye, and they say, 'I'm in trouble. I need you. Can you help me?' You know, we're not afraid of being vulnerable."

As I watched Jane Fonda, always looking so impossibly chic, sitting next to her costars, who were all manifestly touched by what she was saying, my mind immediately went to my dear friend Demond Martin, the person who wrote the book you're holding in your hands right now.

I know this may sound a bit strange because Jane Fonda was delivering a soliloquy on female friendship, but the reason I thought of my dear friend Demond is because he is a man who so clearly embodies everything she was talking about. He is that friend who is always pulling people aside, one after the other, at a big gathering for an eye-to-eye confab to find out what's going on in their lives. He's the one who shows up at our house to sit on the porch with my husband and catch up with no agenda. He's the person who is eager to introduce you to his posse of old pals with whom he has maintained deep and meaningful relationships. Demond is the dude who keeps secrets and gases you up like a football coach with a championship within reach. The one who remembers your kids' names and birthdays and organizes transportation so that the village can show up en masse at a funeral in another state to provide the group hug a grieving friend most surely needs.

Jane Fonda's sermon on female friendship also made me think of how often other men I knew were gathering to gaze outward at sporting events or soaring golf balls or fishing rods or bowling lanes instead of shifting their focus to really look deeply at each other, or even inward at themselves.

Demond is one of the most successful businessmen I know. He's made good choices and strong bets, and as a result, financial reward has flowed in his direction. But his true wealth is measured in other ways, as a husband, father, mentor, and trusted friend. When Demond was thinking about writing a memoir on his incredible life's journey that began on the rough-and-tumble streets of Los Angeles, I shared the story about that Jane Fonda interview because I hoped his strong and steady approach to friendship might form the scaffolding for a book that would help other people flex that emotional muscle in their own lives. What you will see in the following pages is exactly that: a remarkable celebration of how we can all thrive with the power and promise of the quiet magic of friendship.

—Michele Norris

Michele Norris is one of the most trusted voices in American journalism and the author of *Our Hidden Conversations: What Americans Really Think About Race and Identity.*

INTRODUCTION

What Is a Friend of the Good?

New Orleans in July felt like a thousand degrees, but the mood? The mood was good. I was out on the street with my wife, Kia, my cousin Mo, and my team. Thousands of people were walking by, music blasting, street vendors everywhere, the air smelling like beignets. There was so much energy, folks laughing and joyful, everybody vibing. This was ESSENCE Fest, the largest celebration of Black culture and excellence in America, a community of five hundred thousand people. And it was the moment of truth for a product I had put years into developing—years of talking to people about how they succeeded and how they failed. I had spoken to brilliant consumer specialists, merchants and retailers, Wall Street veterans, and executives from corporate America. They were kind enough to share their stories of what went wrong (when they ordered too much inventory, fell short on delivering, or flubbed a product launch) and what went well (when they hit the right note with consumers or hired the perfect manager). Folks were crowded around our booth, sampling an energy drink we were debuting that was designed to be natural, green tea powered, and healthier for our consumers, with less caffeine, fewer calories, and no added sugar. We wanted our energy drink to be a substitute for sugary sodas, which are among the biggest contributors to poor diets in the United States. We could have used artificial sweeteners, which are cheap and do the job without raising the calorie count, but we chose to go natural, making the formula more complex and slightly more expensive. We designed all of our products with deliberate care, prioritizing health and quality while avoiding contributions to issues like diabetes, hypertension, and high cholesterol—challenges that disproportionately impact communities of color. However, I knew that this focus could not compromise taste. "It doesn't matter how good something is for you," Indra Nooyi, the former CEO of PepsiCo, told me. "No one is going to buy it if it doesn't taste good." Which is why we also spent a ton of time formulating the flavors: mango and fruit punch.

This was my first opportunity to engage with people, not just to introduce them to our energy drink but also to share the story of our company, WellWithAll, and our mission to give back to Black, Brown, and underserved communities in more ways than one. As I offered each passerby a half-filled cup, I noticed their smiles and their pride in seeing a Black CEO. When explaining why I founded the company, I talked about my family's health struggles and how those challenges shaped my vision for addressing the support gaps in our healthcare system. I described how I decided to use capitalism as a force for good—that was a new idea for a lot of people, but hearing our story changed their perspective.

When I founded WellWithAll, I walked away from my position as a partner at one of the largest hedge funds in the world, work that had been the final step in taking me and my family from a life of struggle to prosperity. I had done the improbable, overcoming many obstacles, and then after twenty years I decided to change course. I had seen too many family members, people I love dearly, suffer from disease, addiction, and depression because of a combination of poverty, racism, and lack of access to healthcare. I knew that if we hadn't had money and connections, those already difficult journeys would have been impossible. So I started a company that would focus on health and wellness in both the products we sold (supplements, a natural energy drink, a protein powder, and more) and how we handled the profits (by giving 20 percent back to communities with limited access to maternal, heart, and mental healthcare). WellWithAll is a company based on my own experience, not some calculation made by a market research firm or in a corporate boardroom.

ESSENCE Fest was the kind of moment any entrepreneur hopes for—to have their product well received, and not by some focus group being paid $150 an hour to tell you what you want to hear. People who had no reason to tell us anything other than the truth walked by, stopped, sampled, and engaged in conversations. It was a good, honest audience, and they were liking what we were doing. It was like showing your baby to the world: Is he cute? Is he ugly? We were getting feedback, and the feedback was love.

"This is good, man! So good!"

"Wow, that's so cool. Where can I buy this?"

"Are you the CEO?"

"This is your company?!"

All day long I was texting with my WellWithAll cofounder Carmichael Roberts. Every couple of hours, I sent him videos of the crowd's reaction, telling him how unbelievable it all was, and that I was rejoicing in the idea that we had created something special. I also texted Jim Cash, one of my mentors and partners, and I reached out to early investors and friends who had put capital into WellWithAll when it was nothing more than an idea, people who said, "If you're doing this, I'm in."

On the streets of New Orleans, I was sharing this moment with my cousin Mo and his wife, Stacy. Every time I looked at my cousin, I thought of our childhood, our struggles, what we wanted out of life, and the friendship that helped us reach our goals. And now, here he was, seeing what I'd built, seeing that it was something really good. Every once in a while, he'd dap me up and say, "I can't believe all this is happening." The pride on his face was clear, even without him saying a word.

It was overwhelming. My heart was racing. My wife, Kia, had tears streaming down her face. Seeing her in the middle of everything happening around us made tears come to my eyes as well. When I left my investment job, some people doubted me. They said what I wanted to do was risky, unrealistic, overly ambitious. They said I was being emotional. I wasn't. I had been detailed, calculating, and focused on making my plan, as I'd done many, many times before in my life. But building anything new requires a leap of faith, and being surrounded by my community, feeling their love, was an extraordinary moment of pride and validation.

For Kia, it was probably more of a moment of relief. She had absorbed all the stress of this effort. At so many points she'd wondered why I was doing this, what WellWithAll was going to mean for our family in terms of my time, focus, and travel away from home. There was the pressure of my desire and drive to make things different in the world, not just to help a handful of people, which we had always tried to do, but to make a real dent in a system that was doing harm. I wanted to do something big and sustainable. For both of us, these tears were a release of all the emotion from everything we'd been through as a family and now, taking this big swing, building a consumer business that would not only sell great products but use the power of capitalism to turn the tide on a societal wrong.

Standing on this street corner in New Orleans, sweating in this crowd of people, it became real, not just some idea I was telling her about: "Baby, we're going to sell some vitamins, and we're going to do some good in the community." Or "Here's our commercial on Instagram, look at all the likes!" This was one person after another, hundreds and eventually thousands throughout the day, telling us this was good. WellWithAll wasn't just a dream; we had created a real business.

I have always lived my life very privately. I'm not someone who has spent time touting my achievements in person or online. I have been focused on what I could accomplish, how I could (quietly) help, and taking care of my family. But because of my unusual success in the investment world, I was often asked to give talks about my professional path. Eventually I started saying yes, agreeing to share my life story at my alma mater, the University of North Carolina at Charlotte, high schools, churches, and college prep programs. I couldn't ignore the response. Students in particular would come up to me after a talk to tell me what it meant to them to see me and how much they appreciated that I saw their potential to do what I did—to go from a childhood of poverty and limited horizons to my position at a prominent investment firm.

Students want to know how to break into what feels like a secret society. The investment world is an exclusive and tightly controlled network of opportunities. The people who land these coveted jobs tend to come from a small group of institutions. To access them you usually need the "right" internships from the "right" colleges, which lead to the "right" jobs at select firms like Goldman Sachs, and eventually to the "right" business schools, such as Harvard and Stanford. These steps collectively become the golden ticket. But it's not the only way. I let the students know that ultimately there are various paths to reach the same destination, and the key is developing expertise and surrounding yourself with great people you can learn from. Before I landed a job at Adage Capital Management, I was focused on private equity, but even more important than zeroing in on any specific industry was finding someone with a proven track record of consistent leadership and outperformance who knew how to survive in challenging markets and was willing to teach me. Had I stayed rigidly focused on one industry, I might have missed out on an incredible opportunity. The advice I always give is: Build your skills, seek mentorship, and stay open to paths that help you grow—you never know where they might lead.

Students also want to know what it was like to be in these environments. What was the pressure like? Was there racism? Did I ever feel like an impostor? What was it like to be "the only" in the room, and how did I navigate that experience? Sometimes I was asked questions about managing family expectations, balancing the demands of trying to chart my own path, and figuring out how to bring others, those I felt I might be leaving behind, along with me on the ride.

I began to think about writing a book. For ten years I would jot down ideas that felt important to me and lessons of how I navigated through tough times and overcame obstacles in my way. I have been able to achieve financial security and respect in my field due to a lot of hard work, discipline, and what some people call luck, and what I call God's plan. But I also had something else. I had people whom I trusted, with whom I had built solid relationships over the years. These people taught me the core values I lived by and guided key decisions throughout my life. Eventually, looking back, I realized that at every moment of consequence a person was there, someone who was critical to helping me move in the right direction.

The first person to point out the right path to me was my Grannie. Through her acts of kindness, she showed me the joy of giving to others. I had a teacher who made extra time for me in school when I was struggling. My cousin Mo and I shared a vision of what our futures could be beyond the limits of those around us. I had professors and mentors and partners who taught me new skills and showed me the power of my own hard work. And, of course, there is my incredible wife, Kia, my spouse, my life partner, my soulmate. She's also my dearest and closest friend. She sees in me what I see in her.

I considered these people friends, and their friendship was the thing that made the difference between a life of struggle or barely making it and the one that I have—college, business school, boardrooms, family, and community. But those relationships didn't quite fit into the typical mold of what we might think of as friendship.

Aristotle calls these people *friends of the good*. Centuries before Christ's birth, Aristotle's writings on politics, philosophy, science, and the arts made him one of the most influential thinkers in history, but he's less well remembered for his philosophy on friendship, which he viewed as crucial to human happiness and even to human existence itself. I stumbled upon Aristotle's perspective while learning about friendship—reading articles and books, listening to podcasts, whatever I could get my hands on—in search of a framing that best captured what I've observed in my life over the past fifty years. Eventually I found a book called *The Nicomachean Ethics*. That was it. Aristotle had it.

Aristotle described three kinds of friends. He called the first group *friends of utility*. These relationships are built on mutual benefit, where each person provides something the other needs. A friend of utility might ask for a loan when they're short on cash or offer you a ride when your car is in the shop. You study together or collaborate on a group project, dividing up responsibilities. These are transactional connections, practical and functional, but they don't go deep.

These friendships have their place, often in working relationships, but they usually fade away when they stop being profitable or useful.

Then there are what Aristotle calls *friends of pleasure*—someone to party with, meet for a movie, or invite to a pickup basketball game. These friends bring enjoyment, laughs, and amusement into our lives. Friends of pleasure are important—nothing wrong with a good time—but like friends of utility, they are often superficial. For men, this can mean hanging at a bar or a sports game for hours, but the conversation never gets below the surface. Often with these kinds of friends, years can pass, but you still don't really know who they are. And they don't know you.

In fact, both friends of utility and pleasure are temporary, based on fleeting needs. These friendships begin quickly and often break off just as quickly. In book 8 of *The Nicomachean Ethics,* Aristotle wrote, "People who enter into friendly relations quickly have the wish to be friends, but cannot really be friends without being worthy of friendship, and also knowing each other to be so; the wish to be friends is a quick growth, but friendship is not."[1] When a friend of utility is no longer useful, they cease to be a friend. When a friend of pleasure stops being fun because of maturity, changing circumstances, or conflict, the friendship withers. I've had my fair share of these friendships, and they didn't come to mind when I looked back at how I got to where I am.

But there's a third type of friendship, which Aristotle describes as friendship *between the good,* among those "who resemble each other in virtue."[2] These are relationships in which both parties see the good (the virtue) inherent in each other.

Since virtue is permanent, so too are these relationships—they don't wax and wane over time. You may not be in constant touch, but the closeness, respect, and understanding don't fade. It is, he wrote, the "perfect" form of friendship. That's what the people at key moments in my life have in common—they are all friends of the good.

Friends of the good are foundational to this book and one of the secrets to my success in work and in life, but also really relevant to the era we live in. In May 2023, U.S. Surgeon General Vivek Murthy identified loneliness and isolation as an epidemic in our country, three years after the Covid-19 pandemic immobilized the world.[3] Dr. Murthy warned that disconnection and isolation were having severe consequences, and not just on mental health. Loneliness and isolation are contributing factors to increased risk of premature death, heart disease, and stroke. Anxiety, depression, and dementia are the outcomes of our frayed social fabric. Economic consequences aren't abstract either: Lost productivity, lower academic achievement, and workplace absenteeism result. Our economy suffers. Our families suffer. Our health suffers. Our spirits suffer.

Material pursuits aren't the answer. No one lying on their deathbed is thinking, I wish I had bought one more watch, a bigger house, a diamond pinky ring, or two more cars. The collection of extraordinary people who really ride for you, who really love you, who are protective of your relationship, who care for your children, and who will offer their time, talent, and treasure expecting nothing back—those people are worth so much more than any material thing. In a clinical review of nearly 150 studies that collectively included more than three hundred thousand participants, people with strong social connections had a 50 percent better chance of survival compared to those with weaker ties, regardless of age, sex, or health status.[4] It's clear we do better when we connect with one another. We need good friends.

The increase in disconnection is hitting young people especially hard. One survey found that among Gen Zers eighteen to twenty-six years old, only 15 percent described their mental health as excellent. That number was about 50 percent a decade ago.[5] We need to recognize that we live in a moment—especially in Black, Brown, and underserved communities—in which we treat our children's mental health issues the way we used to talk about cancer in the 1960s. It's a source of shame, a challenge that we prefer to keep a dark secret. We talk openly about our kids' achievements but stay silent about their pain and struggles. That needs to change, and we should help kids learn how to cultivate deep friendships in a time when, at best, smartphones are an easy replacement for face-to-face conversations and, at worst, social media creates unrealistic expectations and false appearances.

When I meet young people out in the world, I am concerned about what I see. These days, whether we're walking into a waiting room, standing in line at a coffee shop, or sitting down at a restaurant, it's common to notice people avoiding eye contact, their attention focused on screens. I understand the draw of technology. I am part of several chat groups that keep me in touch with people who live across the country. I even understand the power of online connections through video games and other platforms, especially for anyone who might not feel like they fit in their own communities. The problem is not necessarily the existence of relationships formed online but when online connections completely replace our in-person interactions. It used to be that you needed to go out of your house to meet someone; now anyone can swipe to the next relationship option. On the internet, if a conversation or connection gets complicated—and it easily can, considering the lack of nuance—we can move on to the next thing that is easy or entertaining, whether that's a new person or the next social media post. The thing is, in-person or online, the definition of a friend of the good should still apply—a friend should not disappear when there is a misunderstanding, a difficulty, or an inconvenience. True friendships overcome those complexities; that's how our connections get stronger.

I have seen in my community how men in particular who fail to form deep friendships can become isolated, depressed, and suicidal. The pressure of being a father, a husband, and a provider can be tough, especially when things don't work out as hoped. It's embarrassing to lose a job or to feel like you're falling behind while others rise. Everyone stumbles, but not everyone talks about it. When you're surrounded by people who aren't vulnerable, you start to believe you're the only one struggling, and that isolation grows.

According to the American Institute for Boys and Men, the suicide rate for men has increased 40 percent over the past two decades and is four times the suicide rate of women.[6] Suicide has a complex set of causes, but it's hard not to see some link to the difficulty men seem to have forming and maintaining meaningful friendships.

As the leader of the men's ministry at my church for more

than five years, I've seen and talked men through these pressures. From my own experience, there's a part of me shaped by the struggles of my childhood that still flickers with fear. It's the shadow of a dream, a passing thought, a persistent worry: What if I fail? What if I end up back in poverty? What if I disappoint the people who rely on me? These fears, though quiet, have a way of surfacing, reminding me of the stakes and the weight of responsibility I carry. That weight is heavy, and at times it feels like it could crush me.

In the early days of a family health crisis, I had no idea how to handle it. I didn't think many people I knew had faced something like what we were dealing with. I wondered who to tell, what to say, and how to work through it. Deciding to be vulnerable and share what our family was dealing with turned out to be one of the best decisions of my life. Kia was the main driver behind that honesty—she encouraged us to be open with family and friends, not to pretend everything was okay.

That choice saved me so much heartache. It opened the door for other people to say, "I've been through the same thing—here's what we did, here are the mistakes we made." There's a relief that comes with realizing you're not the only one. Before that, it felt like I was going to explode on the inside every day, surrounded by people I loved but not sharing my struggles. Even when you don't say anything, people know when something's off. You feel like a fraud, not being genuine with yourself or those you care about. Some burdens are just too heavy to carry alone. That was a huge lesson for me: No matter how skilled I am, there are many things I simply can't do by myself.

This is why it's critical to have a crew around you, a space where these fears can be spoken aloud and the irrational thoughts confronted. You can talk with a friend of the good about the most painful, personal things in your life. When you can talk about your pain, you're bearing the fullness of that pain rather than hiding it. And when you're able to bear it, the pain can be healed instead of repressed. As men, we often push our feelings down, avoid, put on a brave face, and bear our pain alone. Often, we don't realize the value of being vulnerable with friends. And later in life regret not sharing more of our struggles.

While this isn't a book exclusively for men, I believe men—especially Black and Brown men and the people who love them—stand to gain the most from it. Men need to find a new language to express themselves. When we say we need or want *someone who has our back,* most often we're really looking for someone to be at our side with empathy, with faith, with kindness. That's hard to admit.

My life has been blessed beyond my wildest dreams. To the best of my knowledge, I was the first Black partner at a major hedge fund in America. This has brought financial security that, as a young adult, I did not believe was possible. I've been married to someone I consider a dear friend for close to thirty years and we have two beautiful children. Now I have started a new business and found more ways to give back to society.

Some people who pick up this book might expect a story about a poor Black kid who pulls himself up by his bootstraps. A lucky kid with smarts and good values and a strong work ethic who transforms himself into a self-made multimillionaire. A shining example of how free markets and capitalism turn talented Americans into rich Americans—an uplifting morality tale about America and rugged individualism.

That would be complete bull. This is not that book, and I am not that person. The secret to my success isn't what people expect to hear. It's not about vision or drive or work ethic, though obviously those are parts of it. My achievements are largely the result of necessary interventions from people interwoven into my life who have helped, guided, and supported me at key points. This book, and my story, is one of mutual aid, collective responsibility, and moral guidance. The superman mentality is just hubris. If you think you can make it alone, you've been set up for massive failure. You need a community of friends to have a full and joyful life.

So, what are we really looking for in our friendships? People who will stick with us so that we're not alone when life falls apart. Too often, we think someone has our back, but it turns out they're just a transactional friend or a friend of pleasure. The folks who were showing up for my parties, coming over for Thanksgiving, or hanging out when I had something going on, like a golf tournament, men's dinner, or special music performance—where were they when tragedy struck? When I was living through that pain, who showed up? Who said, "Hey, I'll come over for an hour" or "Let me just sit with you" or "Do you guys need food? How can I pray for you?"

When a loved one of mine was in the hospital, the bishop from our church walked there every day for six months.

Every day he walked, in the snow, in the rain. It was not a one-time thing. Someone who shows up day after day, prays day after day, that's a friend of the good.

Friends of the Good tells the stories of the most important people in my life: those who showed up, guided me, cared for me, and invested in my success and happiness. I'm blessed to have far more close friendships than the number of chapters, but the ones I chose represent archetypes that anyone can recognize—a wise elder, teacher, brother, partner, mentor or sponsor, or ride or die. While they all share similar attributes, they reveal who they are in different ways and at different stages in my life—how they helped me and continue to help me. Each one bestowed upon me lessons that I have carried throughout my life. And they all strive to be incredibly helpful to a lot of people. They want to do good by being good. One reader might identify a single archetype of friends of the good in their life. Another might spot five. Another might have all of them. The important thing is not the number but the quality of those friendships.

One of the most important goals of *Friends of the Good* is to offer practical advice on how to *identify, maintain,* and *be* friends of the good. Sometimes friends of the good are right in front of us, but we don't see them. Sometimes you need to seek them out. And when we find them, whether around the family dinner table, in a classroom, in a house of worship, or on the other end of the phone line, friends of the good don't automatically remain a part of our lives unless we do the work of maintaining those friendships. There are no one-way relationships—generosity and kindness received must be met with generosity and kindness given in return. Like my grandmother and my elementary schoolteacher, a friend of the good sometimes plays a role that can't be immediately reciprocated. In that case, a friend of the good can pay that debt forward to another child, to another grandparent, maybe to a stranger.

My best mentors have never pointed to a road and said, "This is a path I took, so this is the path you should take." Instead, they counseled, "This is what I learned from my path. Take from it what you can." This book is written in the same way. It's not a self-help book; it's an honest story of my life and its lessons, and it's about the people who have stood at every threshold to hold my hand as they steered me toward a path that I might not have seen without them. This is a book about the trials and triumphs I've experienced from childhood to parenthood, from poverty to prosperity, and from being on my own to being part of a community of one of the most powerful forces available to all of us: friends of the good.

CHAPTER 1

Miss Polly

Giver

Miss Polly, my Grannie, was the first friend of the good in my life. She gave me foundational love. Every time I came into her house, she would light up, always making me feel like I was bringing her joy. That consistency and love gave me confidence. She also gave me a whole treasure trove of life lessons—wisdom passed down from an elder like an heirloom—showing me what compassion, generosity, and kindness looked like. She was a friend of the good long before I even knew what that meant. Grannie showed me that giving isn't just an act of generosity. It's a sign of our humanity.

When I was growing up in Columbus, Ohio, my grandmother Polly had a nickname for me: "Money." (I had a side hustle selling candy when I was seven or eight years old, but more on that later.) Back then, when I danced through the door of her house, she'd hug me tight and fuss over me like I'd been gone for months, even if I had seen her just that morning. "Money," she'd say, "come on in here, boy. Dinner's ready. Go wash your hands."

Grannie was a tough, skinny woman with a big personality. She was a churchgoer who cussed a ton, talked a lot of trash, enjoyed a bit of snuff under her gums in the afternoon, and kept a gun in the house. She was charismatic and funny as hell. Her jokes kept us rolling on the floor (literally), and she was always jabbing at people. She'd say, "What IS that outfit?" or "Have you gained a little weight?" Her house was full of laughter and joy, but she didn't suffer fools. You did not screw around with Grannie.

Miss Polly was born Polly Ann Harding on August 1, 1919, in Yadkin County, North Carolina. She had six brothers and sisters—Odell (also known as Buddy), Warren, Nelson, John, Mary, and Will. She didn't have much while growing up and didn't talk about her childhood, although she did tell me about going to school with Great-Uncle Buddy's future wife, Great-Aunt Mella, and "whooping her ass" every day. Grannie loved to tell stories like that. I'm not sure if they were all true. She eventually married and had two children, my Aunt Sue and my dad, Thomas. In North Carolina, she washed other people's laundry to make money for her family.

After Grannie separated from my grandfather, she moved from North Carolina to Columbus, Ohio, to live with her brother John and his wife. She lived with them when her brother became sick with severe diabetes, helping them around the house whenever they needed anything. Cooking, cleaning, you name it, Grannie was there to lend a hand. My

Great-Uncle John, like many in the African American community, was not properly treated and unfortunately had to have his leg amputated. Grannie's presence helped her brother adjust to life as an amputee, especially after his wife died. When he died, he left her his house.

Grannie went to Columbus to be a source of support to her sister-in-law and brother until the end of their lives and was gifted a home, so she used that space to take care of renters who might have had trouble finding housing elsewhere. The people she rented out spare rooms to were polite, down-on-their-luck older men. The renters kept the rooming house neat and quiet. Grannie knew life was hard and sometimes people needed a break and some kindness. She was constantly at the stove cooking up fried chicken, biscuits, and on occasion chitlins. When she wasn't putting food on the table, she canned tomatoes and fruit to give away to people who didn't have enough to eat. She was a beacon of light for me and those around us, and one of the most generous people I knew as a kid.

My early years in Columbus were a comfortable and happy time in my childhood. I had a close relationship with both of my parents. My dad had a successful tow truck business, while my mom, Rita, had a well-paid factory job. Sometimes Dad would let me ride around with him in his truck, propped up on pillows in the passenger seat so I could see over the dashboard. My family had a three-bedroom house with a garage and a backyard on a tree-lined street. As in many Black households, plastic protected the living room furniture so that no one would jack up the fabric, and no one could ever sit down, at least not comfortably. For many of the years we lived there, in the late 1970s and early 1980s, we were the only Black family on the block, but we got along with our neighbors.

Both of my parents worked long hours. At one point, my dad employed three or four people, and I thought of him as an entrepreneur. He was on call twenty-four hours a day, with a work ethic that left a lasting impression on me. Then there was my mother, who worked a variety of factory jobs, often on the night shift. She was a Black woman without the advantages of higher education in male-dominated jobs, which limited her opportunities. Both of my parents worked incredibly hard, but it was different. For my mom, it was depleting and unsatisfying. For my dad, running his own business and being his own boss gave him a sense of joy, fulfillment, and a degree of freedom. Sure, he could be called at any moment, but I remember how he was able to show up for me: buying me a white dirt bike, teaching me to drive a dump truck, and sharing his love of tinkering with cars.

I grew up basically as an only child. I had a sister, Tonia, who was five years older than me and two brothers, Ronnie and Craig, who were twelve and fifteen years older, respectively. My brothers and sister were from my father's previous marriages, but they weren't considered "half" siblings. I idolized my older brothers, especially Ronnie, who was tall and really good at basketball. My sister lived with us for a little while when she was in high school, and she'd help look after me. Her friends would come over, and I would entertain them by breakdancing and telling jokes. We'd play around and have a lot of fun together, but for the most part, my older siblings would come and go. So, when my parents were working, I spent a lot of time bouncing between Grannie's house and my cousins who lived nearby, which was fine by me.

Grannie's house was across town near a housing project. It was a big, rambling house with a porch in front. Her bedroom was downstairs off the kitchen. Upstairs was where the short-term renters stayed, always coming and going. I watched how Grannie interacted with the men in her house. There was always a plate of food ready to be given, and she was a voice of wisdom as she listened to their problems. She was firm when she needed to be. She was no fool. I remember overhearing someone ask Grannie for money. She said no and then under her breath said to herself, *That guy is full of shit*. Grannie taught me to read people, understand them, be generous, and be smart about it.

The candy side hustle I mentioned included selling Lemonheads, Red Hots, Hot Tamales, and lollipops out of my backpack to make extra pocket change. The school bus was my first entrepreneurial opportunity. I would spend some of what I made, save some, and sometimes I would give loans to Grannie's boarders, a couple of bucks to tide them over between paychecks. That was how Grannie came up with my nickname. I was a little grade-school banker, doling out cash when someone needed help.

It wasn't all business for me and Grannie; some afternoons we'd sit together and watch soap operas, or "the stories," as she called them, like *Days of Our Lives*. There was Bo and Hope's romance and the villain Victor Kiriakis, a shady businessman. It might not have been something that a little kid should have been watching, but in a strange way it allowed me to see circumstances very different from what was in my everyday life. On TV there were mansions and fancy cars and luxurious vacations. It was also just fun to watch the drama play out and hear Grannie's commentary on the storylines.

During my time with Grannie, she and I baked together—pound cake was one of our favorites. We'd measure out three cups of flour, three gigantic cups of sugar, a ton of butter, a few eggs, milk, salt, vanilla, baking powder, and a little bit of lemon zest. At first, I'd watch her while we stood side by side at the counter, me standing on a step stool. After a while, as I learned, she watched me bake. I remember the wonderful buttery smell coming from the oven. We would sit down to fresh-cut slices, still warm, and eat them with glasses of milk.

Whatever she was doing, I was hanging around. While she cleaned or prepared meals to hand out, I watched TV or played with jacks, sticks, and balls. It wasn't like there were any real video games back then. Grannie spent a lot of time working on quilts, and at some point I got interested. She gathered scraps of fabric from old clothes and blankets or leftover bits that on their own could have been mistaken for trash, and by weaving them together with love and care, Grannie turned them into a masterpiece of colorful lines and shapes.

Grannie would sit there for hours sewing, and I'd help with the stuffing, hand her needles, and, eventually, learn how to sew. She would give the finished quilts away on special occasions—a new baby, a birthday—or as a gift to someone she just wanted to bless with something nice. People would come to her house to receive their quilt, which Grannie would have folded neatly. Her quilts were puffy and heavy; it was hard to turn over when you were sleeping under one. She'd give a quilt with love and then watch the person's face as they received it. They loved it every time.

Seeing Grannie give her quilts away was the first time I witnessed someone regularly blessing other people with a gift that was really meaningful and had taken months of work. This was not something I saw anyone else doing. That clicked in my brain: She was putting so much effort into something she wasn't getting paid for, doing it out of kindness and getting joy in return. She was giving these presents, and pieces of her heart, just because. It didn't have to be Christmas to do something nice for someone else.

One of the things that has been so special about writing this book is that when I got to the heart of it and started thinking about the influences in my life, I realized how much I had internalized what Grannie taught me about being generous and loving to others. Throughout my life, as a kid and as an adult, I would hear people say, "Miss Polly is amazing, a great cook, a kind lady." I never heard anyone say anything bad about her, and family and friends were always coming to see her to have a laugh and get a little love.

As my grandmother got older and slowed down, you could see how many people cared about her. Whenever I visited her, there were always three or four people on her porch or in her living room, keeping her company. She'd be telling them jokes, and she'd greet me with "Money!," something she called me until she died. When she passed away, her funeral was packed with friends, family, and neighbors. She lived her whole life helping people with no expectations in return, but she got a lot back.

In many cultures the wisdom of elders is cherished, as it should be, but sometimes we don't pay attention and miss out. A study published in 2018 found that strong grandparent-grandchild relationships reduce depressive symptoms in both the child and the grandparents.[1] The study found these relationships offer unconditional love, wisdom, and a sense of community. Grannie gave me all that. Spending so much time with someone selfless and witnessing how she made a big impact on people's lives—that was my introduction to a friend of the good who was a giver.

If we are lucky enough to have access to grandparents, we benefit from spending time hanging out in their kitchens and living rooms, soaking in lessons from their lives. That kind of community between generations is good for everyone, young people at the beginning of their life's adventure and older people who still feel curious and interested in how the world is changing. I'm sort of in the middle now, not so young that there are a lot of wise elders around and not quite ready to take on the role of wise elder myself, but I look for opportunities to do a little bit of both, and I keep learning from those who have lived many decades longer than me.

In the summer of 2025, WellWithAll released a documentary called *Black Longevity* at the Martha's Vineyard African American Film Festival. In it seven people—three incredible couples and a woman named Ruth who is 106—share the secrets to their long and happy lives, which as you might guess has a lot to do with finding joy and giving back. I've watched this film at least thirty times and every time, I feel Grannie's spirit.

One of the couples in the film is Walter Beach and Gail Boyd. Walter, now ninety-three years old, is a sweet soul who is also strong, brilliant, and full of grace. He was an NFL star in the 1960s, but to get there, he had to survive some harrowing experiences. As a child, he went to visit family in the South. On the playground one day, a bunch of kids, Black and white, were racing each other. One of the white kids said there was no way a "nigger" could be faster than a white kid. So Walter and that kid raced each other. Walter won, which led to a fight. When the fight was over, the kids were fine, they had worked it out, but later word spread that the Ku Klux Klan was on its way to pick up Walter and lynch him. His relatives put him in a dress and scurried him out of town, helping him escape.

Walter and Gail have been married for decades, and their life together is a remarkable example of love and companionship, which has propelled them through the years. But their lives aren't just about their relationship—they also have a deep sense of purpose in serving their community. After his NFL career, Walter dedicated his entire life to mentoring young people, supporting youth empowerment and education, and advocating for racial justice. Gail focused on supporting families, Black cultural awareness, and wellness. The way they live as wise elders and givers is so similar to Grannie's path, influencing my life back then and now.

Seeing Grannie help folks through the early years of my life planted a seed in me to do the same. So many people have never been given an opportunity to be successful. You can see brilliance fade in the face of systems that are designed to hold them back. Grannie passed away in 2008, so her friendship is not one I can maintain or repay, but I can carry forward what she gave to me. As I grapple with these gigantic societal issues—health, equity, education, opportunity—I think of Walter and Gail. And I think of Grannie.

In 2016, my wife, Kia, and I started the Martin Scholars Program at the University of North Carolina at Charlotte to fill financial gaps for a group of students—forty so far. We started the program to provide for kids who grew up the way Kia and I did, kids whose parents might not have gone to college or don't have the time, resources, or knowledge to guide them. We try to give them what they need to be successful in college, which includes financial support, but also more than that. When they're coming from poverty, even the brightest of students can end up, for a variety of reasons, having to drop out. So we set up the program to identify supertalented, thoughtful young people who had come from some of the most challenging economic circumstances and help them through. The way Grannie looked out for others who didn't always have what they needed—offering a meal, a place to stay, a sympathetic ear—was a model for us.

Grannie was a great listener. It didn't matter if we were baking or sewing, she'd listen to me and I'd listen to her. These were the moments when we learned from each other and about each other. One of the things that Kia and I do is build real relationships with the scholars and spend time with them. We get to know what they're interested in and hear more about some of the challenges they face.

A key component for them to succeed is exposure, not just in terms of college but in the world beyond. When *Hamilton* was superhot on Broadway, we took all the scholars to New York. One day a student reached out to a chaperone in distress. They realized someone had been in their room while they were out. When they left, they said, their blinds were open and their bed was made, and when they came back, the covers were turned down, there were two chocolates on the bed, and the curtains were closed. They had never stayed in a hotel before, so they hadn't experienced turndown service. Most had not been to restaurants that weren't chains and had never seen a Broadway musical. Those exposures gave some texture to their lives, and the experiences will help them in interviews, boardrooms, and when they travel, for work or pleasure, later in life. And through these experiences we see them blossom.

We've been blessed to support students who are Black and white, straight and gay, and from all sorts of ethnic heritages and backgrounds. The thing they have in common is their desire to make a significant contribution to society in their chosen fields and to their families financially. They are often the first in their families to go to college. Many of them have experienced heartache, pain, and mental or physical health issues. Some have lost their parents before coming to school or while in school. And these kids, these young adults, persevere in such extraordinary ways. Like Grannie, they have taught me about toughness and grit, and I have felt incredible joy being with them.

Martin Scholars go on to become accountants, entrepreneurs, architects, and nurses, get their PhDs and receive awards—each working to make the world a little bit better. One of our students, Bryan, got into the Summer Venture in Management Program at Harvard Business School, an experience that was so instrumental in changing my life. To see him thriving in that program was really, really cool. Another scholar, Anthony, an extraordinary human who graduated with a 4.0 GPA, called me when he was trying to decide between job offers, so I introduced him to a few people. The job he ended up taking was at a much bigger company than he initially was going to choose, with a lot more responsibility than he had expected. He's doing great there now. With a phone call, I was able to change the trajectory of how he could apply his talents. That doesn't happen for most of us, but that's exactly what happened for me and why I want to do it for others.

The Martin Scholars has been one of our single greatest philanthropic investments because it keeps on giving. These scholarships are meaningful not just because of what the students accomplish after college but also because of how I see them supporting one another, continuing the tradition of giving. When Kia and I go back to campus, at least a few times a year, we meet with the current scholars along with their older counterparts who come back to share information about what they are doing and give advice—wise elders, but not that old. I have seen the Martin Scholars grow from individuals into a community.

In 2024, I was humbled to receive an award from the U.S. Dream Academy alongside Oprah Winfrey, but the proudest moment of the night for me was when MaKena, a Martin

Scholar, stood onstage in front of thousands of people and introduced me.

She talked through some of the accomplishments on my résumé, but that's not what got to me. She said, "Here's what I know about him. He is generous and kind and embodies all that is good in people. His presence makes you feel comfortable, even in moments like this. As I prepare to graduate from UNC Charlotte's Business Honors Program, he still stands as a source of inspiration. And a reminder to get my shoulders ready for the next generation." It was an overwhelming moment for me. I couldn't stop crying. Grannie taught me to be a giver. Now I was seeing the impact shining through MaKena, who along with the other Martin Scholars gave me immense hope for the future. This was Grannie's gift coming around full circle.

Chapter 1 Insights

- Unconditional love creates confidence that lasts a lifetime. Seek out those who light up when you enter a room and make you feel valued simply for being yourself.
- Observe and absorb the wisdom of elders—their lived experiences offer invaluable life lessons that can't be found in textbooks or online.
- True giving isn't just about material things but about sharing your time, skills, wisdom, and presence. Like Grannie's quilts, small acts of generosity create beautiful patterns in others' lives.

- Intergenerational relationships benefit everyone involved. Studies show they reduce depression and create a sense of community and continuity.
- Carry forward the gifts you've received by becoming a giver yourself. The impact of generosity multiplies across generations, creating ripples of positive change.

CHAPTER 2

Mom and Miss Johns

Strength-Finders

Miss Johns was a friend of the good who was a teacher. She helped me find my strengths and overcome my weaknesses in school. She gave me the confidence to set goals for myself that were different from what I saw around me—a lot of violence and despair—and to use education as a tool to forge a path to success and freedom.

I never would have found Miss Johns if it wasn't for my mom and her fierce commitment to education. Despite difficult circumstances, she did everything she could to set me on the right path. That focus became the foundation for my survival and eventual success. Together, they showed me a way forward when the world around me seemed intent on pulling me down.

"I should smoke that fool."

I froze when I heard those words. I knew the guy speaking

was talking about me. I was playing my favorite arcade game in a convenience store in Inglewood, California. It was a regular corner shop with rows of potato chips and a cooler with malt liquor and soda. I was trying to stay alive in the game when I heard the jingle of the door opening behind me. Between all the shelved goods and the arcade games tucked in a far corner of the store, there were only three customers—the two guys who'd just walked in and me. I didn't really think anything about it until I heard those words.

I was eleven years old, probably not more than five feet tall and a hundred pounds, wearing my favorite outfit—a bright red tracksuit. What I didn't know was, at that time in the early 1980s, there were two main gangs in L.A.: the Crips and the Bloods. The Bloods wore red. Red like my tracksuit.

I kept playing, my eyes fixed on the screen as my heart raced. "He's just a little kid," the second guy said. Then the jingle rang again, and they walked out onto the sidewalk. I sighed with relief. I was safe. For the moment.

Inglewood, just a short distance from Los Angeles International Airport, was nothing like the L.A. in TV shows like *Beverly Hills, 90210*. It also wasn't like anywhere I knew growing up, nothing like Columbus, Ohio, where I had spent ten comfortable years, and nothing like North Carolina, where I went during the summers to visit my cousins. My experience of Inglewood was similar to the depictions of L.A. in later movies like *Training Day* and *Boyz n the Hood*—riddled with gangs and drugs. And now, it was my home.

My mom moved us to Inglewood about two years after my parents got divorced. One of her brothers lived there, and while they weren't particularly close, she had little support in

Columbus, and she wanted to try something new. She was optimistic, believing that uprooting our lives and replanting us in Los Angeles would be a new beginning in the land of opportunity. My dad cried when I left, which was one of only two times I saw him cry in my life. The other time was when Grannie died.

My parents' marriage had broken up the summer before I entered third grade. They just weren't getting along. In hindsight, I realize my mother was deeply depressed throughout my childhood, but as a kid I would have said that my mom was sad a lot.

Like me, my mom was never diagnosed as dyslexic, but she struggled to spell and read quickly. When she was growing up, in the 1950s and 1960s, schools didn't recognize or make adjustments for students who struggled. They were just considered bad students or not very smart. My mother felt that her brothers, who were so light-skinned they could nearly pass for white, had opportunities she did not. They seemed to move through society socially in a much easier way, while my mom had to fight for everything she got. Like my Grannie, she had a grit and determination that sustained her, but many challenges impacted my mom's self-esteem and what she was able to achieve.

Unfortunately, my mom wasn't in a great position economically once we settled in Inglewood. My dad sent some money to help, but it wasn't always enough. Sometimes we'd run out of money. There were times when we'd be short on food or the electric company would shut off the apartment lights. She had a wide variety of jobs, and we moved around a lot. There was already so much weight on her shoulders as a

Black woman, and it intensified once we were on our own in California. My mom did the best she could. Her father never gave her much support, and her mother, who by all accounts was wonderful and held the family together, died when I was a baby. My mother was also very close to her sister, Norma. They were best friends. As a kid, I remember Norma having such life, joy, and strength. Then she got sick. She was a key support for my mom but died young, around the time of my parents' divorce. The situation was stressful, and it's understandable that my mom may have wanted someone to take care of her. Mom got involved with two men who were charming and charismatic but, unfortunately, also violent. The first was Malik.

We lived with Malik in a housing project everyone called "the Jungle," an appropriate name for a living situation where there was real danger and uncertainty. Malik was a big bald guy—he seemed gigantic to me. I remember once when Malik and my mom were fighting, my mom sent me outside. I was throwing a ball with a neighbor, when the fight between my mom and Malik erupted into the street. I tried to intervene, but I wasn't big enough or strong enough to help her. Malik pushed me away as he slapped and punched my mom. No one stopped him. I looked at the man I was playing ball with, hoping he would do something, but he just turned his eyes down and walked away, leaving us alone in the chaos. These fights continued. Malik hit me, too, sometimes. I don't know if that was the last straw for my mom, but I know she had been working to save enough money to leave, and eventually we did.

About a year later, after I spent a summer in North Carolina, there was a new man in my mom's life. They picked me up at the airport together.

"This is my husband, Paul," she told me. "We fell in love and got married." My mother had been working at a drug rehabilitation clinic. That's where she met Paul, a recovering heroin addict. Paul wasn't quite as mean as Malik. He was smarter and entrepreneurial; he was trying to start a cookie business. He had two kids about my age who didn't live with us, but sometimes we played basketball or shared a meal. We had some fun times together. I remember going to Paul's sister's house for a Christmas party and being given a bottle of cologne. The scene at their house was different from what I was experiencing—they were somewhat affluent—and getting a gift of any type for any reason felt good.

But, sadly, my mom's bad luck returned. Paul's business failed, and he started using drugs again. One time, I was getting on the bus and looked down the street to see Paul, high out of his mind, getting arrested by some cops. I got on the bus and rode off without doing or saying anything. They broke up and we moved on.

Living through the pain and chaos these men brought into our lives made me more determined to make sure that later in life I would not be dependent on others. I believe my mom would not have been in those relationships if she hadn't needed financial and emotional support. In retrospect, seeing my mother disrespected over and over again heightened my awareness of the mistreatment many women face. Difficult experiences can either perpetuate cycles of behavior or become foundations for empathy and change. I committed not only to never inflict the hurt my mother endured but to actively demonstrate respect for women in both my personal and my professional worlds. I strive to truly see the women in my life with open eyes and full recognition. Women are an often-undervalued source of talent, and I've witnessed firsthand how the women in my organization and on my teams provide us with a genuine competitive advantage. When I walk into a business meeting dominated by men, it feels fundamentally wrong. I find myself wondering, *Why aren't there women here?* If there's anything I can do to support and elevate women, I will always step forward.

My mom was protective: She didn't let me go anywhere if she could help it. She tried to keep me from being out in the streets, where, on any given day, I would see fights, guns, bullets flying. Violence—and the fear of violence—was a constant for me. It wasn't enough just to mind your business or avoid trouble; sometimes trouble came looking for you. Gangs were everywhere, recruiting kids who didn't want to join, forcing them into "families" for protection. If you weren't part of one of those families, you risked getting beat up, shoved, kicked around, or worse. I saw people get pulled in, either for protection or for money, because there weren't a lot of other opportunities. I also witnessed and experienced the racism faced by poor folks of color—schools that were overcrowded and chaotic, more than one generation of a family living together in poverty because of a lack of job opportunities. There was a general atmosphere of fear and stifled potential, a reality later reported by rap groups like N.W.A.

Basketball gave me an out, a way to stay on the edges of that world without getting pulled into it. I carried a basketball with me everywhere I went. Dribble, dribble, crossover. I had a nice point guard game for a middle schooler, which gave me a certain level of respect and camaraderie with kids wherever we were living. I could always join a pickup game. It wasn't a perfect shield, but it helped.

At the end of the day, my mother always did what she thought was right for me. As much as you try, you can't truly understand what it means to be a parent until you become one. It's easy to sit on the sidelines, throwing out judgment and criticism. My mom gave everything she could, all her effort, to make a better life for me than the one she had.

What was constant was my mom's hopes for me. She used to tell me that on the day I was born, when she looked at me for the first time, something stirred deep inside her. She thought, *This child is going to be great.* She reinforced that belief in me over and over again. I'd hear it from her so often: "You're going to be great. You're going to do something special." And when she looked at me, I could see it in her eyes. She believed it. No one can give you inner strength the way a parent can.

I was sure that the only shot I would ever have to get rich in Inglewood would come from the McDonald's on my bus route to school. This was back when Mickey D's had its Monopoly instant-winner game. Once or twice a week, if I had an extra dollar, I would jump down from the bus and walk to Mickey D's for a Sausage McMuffin or an apple pie that came with Monopoly game tokens. I'd eat my breakfast and then I'd pull off the stickers, hoping my tokens added up to a winning combination that would turn me into a millionaire. I dreamed about how it would change my life and my mother's life. No more fear, abuse, and violence. We'd be safe. I was always disappointed. I thought it was our only way out, but that was before I met Miss Johns, a teacher at Inglewood Christian School.

At first, I was enrolled in the local public elementary school close to home. Back in Columbus, I went to Catholic schools, where the curriculum was challenging. Even though I couldn't spell well, that academic preparation made public school in Inglewood seem easy—the school was so far behind. There wasn't a lot of discipline or academic rigor. I completed my assignments, didn't make any trouble, and got along with everybody, so relative to the other kids I was seen as a superstar.

After a few months, my mom visited my school for a parent-teacher conference. When she entered the classroom, she found me bent over a stack of papers at one of the desks. She asked the teacher what I was doing. "Grading papers," the teacher told her, as if it were the most natural thing in the world for me to be acting as a teacher's assistant. I don't fully remember, but I'd probably been given the task to keep me busy while my teacher was occupied. But it became crystal clear to my mom that I had to go to a different school. If I was far enough ahead of the other kids to grade their papers, I obviously wasn't being challenged. The reality was actually worse than that. I wasn't learning much at all, coasting through the work, which for my mother was a crisis.

My mother ingrained in me that education was the key to success. Between long shifts and pockets of sleep, she did all that she could to engage my interest in learning. I have great memories of her reading me books, talking in funny voices, creating characters, and encouraging me to care about my education. Back in Columbus my mom would use any free time she had to take me to a museum or a park. Or she would find an interesting movie to bring me to. She wanted to expose me to a bigger, broader world.

In Inglewood she didn't have as much time or money to do those kinds of things with me, but she still invested in my education. We'd go to the library together on weekends, and at home we'd look through our copy of the *Ebony Pictorial History of Black America* together. She didn't want me to have the mental barriers that so many people develop because of their surroundings, so she'd make sure I saw examples of Black excellence and success. At school, in history class, slavery was the only thing we learned about the Black experience. She wanted me to know about the positives, the people who looked like me and came from circumstances like ours who had gone on to achieve great things.

She wanted me to go to college, an opportunity she didn't have. She had worked hard her whole life, never really getting ahead. She didn't want that for me. She wanted more, and I wanted more too. I wanted something better, something different. Even though there weren't a lot of people around me going to college when I was growing up, I always knew I would go because my mom always talked about college as a natural progression for me: "When you go to college," she would say when we talked about my future.

A few days after the parent-teacher conference, Mom took me to a small school called Inglewood Christian. It took a lot of courage for her to pull me out of one school, only a few months in, and enroll me in another, where I would be starting late, but that was how important education was to her. That was the strength-finder moment for me. Without it, I'm not sure anything else in my life would have worked out. By some standards, I was doing well enough at the public school, but there's no chance I would have thought of myself academically the same way if my mom hadn't made that decision.

Inglewood Christian was attached to a church in what looked like a converted two-story motel. The school had an assessment exam to gauge where incoming students stood academically. Despite my position as teacher's assistant at the public school, the holes in my academic achievement were revealed in the assessment. Reading in particular was a struggle for me. I remember sitting in class back in Columbus, waiting to read a passage from a book out loud in front of everyone, which was a common activity in elementary school. As the task moved around the room, I'd try to anticipate my paragraph so I could review it in advance and avoid stumbling when it was my turn. Even now, I practice like that. It's rare for me to go into anything unprepared. I realized later in life, when one of my kids was diagnosed, that I am probably dyslexic, which helped me connect the dots about that possibility for my mom too.

During the assessment, this weakness and other gaps in my abilities were revealed. I was told I would have to repeat the fifth grade, despite having already started sixth grade. I cried from shame and embarrassment. But my mom's push to change schools and this step back turned out to be one of the best things that ever happened to me because of my new fifth-grade teacher.

Inglewood Christian was a small school with only fifteen

to eighteen kids per grade, about half the size of my previous class at the public school. Socially I adjusted quickly, making friends after a few games of four square in the central yard during my first week or so. My teacher, Miss Johns, was young, probably in her late twenties, not a veteran teacher, but she saw my potential even though I was a slow reader. I never thought of myself as a bad student overall, but I did get by in part by being the class clown. A well-placed joke can distract a room from what you don't know, but Miss Johns didn't let me slide. She made me take myself seriously academically. On the weekends, I'd meet Miss Johns at school, and she'd tutor me for free.

Miss Johns helped me discover that I was excellent at math. I had always liked math because I liked business, thanks to my dad, and I liked money. My dad taught me that if you like money, you have to know how to add it up and make sure it doesn't disappear. As my skills improved, so did my confidence in all academics. Suddenly the kid who had to repeat the fifth grade was one of the top math students in the school. I began to have discipline, doing my homework and extra math problems. Miss Johns did not deny that I read slowly; she helped me improve and told me that I was gifted in other subjects. It was a key lesson for me: I didn't have to be good at everything. We should not have a narrow view of intelligence. Miss Johns made me an interested student. School became my armor and my opportunity.

I started dating girls in the grade above me, and one in particular motivated me to try to catch up to my previous grade level, which I did. After seventh grade I was headed to Inglewood High, where I planned to try out for the basketball team. But before my freshman year, after a summer with my dad, who had moved to North Carolina full-time, I realized that I could not go back to Inglewood. There was too much violence, too much instability, too many ways for trouble to find me. The odds of survival, let alone achievement, were low for young Black men. Before that moment, I hadn't really thought about whether I could change my situation. I hadn't discussed how bad it was with my dad. My life in Inglewood was just . . . my life, and I had to figure my way through it. But with the confidence I had built in my abilities, I decided something had to change. So, after my summer in North Carolina, I asked my dad if I could stay. He said yes.

My mom was crushed, but I thought moving was the only way I'd survive my high school years. Even though she was heartbroken, she did not put up a fight. She knew it was the right thing to do for my education. In my sophomore year, my mom moved back east to ensure that I was on track as a student and even moved back in with my dad. It was a sacrifice for both of them because they were not in love, but they would live together in the same house because they thought it was better for me. It was not a choice they would have otherwise made. After I graduated from high school, they went their separate ways again.

By ninth grade, my mom and Miss Johns had given me everything I needed to be successful in high school. By helping me to find my strengths as a student and as a person, my mom and Miss Johns enabled me to take control of my life. This was clear a few months into my new school in North Carolina, when the principal finally received my transcript from Inglewood Christian. He pulled me aside in the hallway and said, "Wait a minute, you skipped eighth grade?" "True," I told him. Thanks to Miss Johns, at that point I had all A's in my freshman classes and never looked back. I never said goodbye to Miss Johns when I left Inglewood, but about fifteen years ago I called to give her an update and to say thank you.

Back in fifth grade, Miss Johns told me I was good at math, but she also told me when I wasn't working hard enough or living up to my potential. I am a firm believer in the importance of correction with love. We need to lift people up, encourage them, and point out the things they do well, but it doesn't do anyone any good to say everything they do is fantastic. There is no growth in that. And we all need to grow and improve in some way.

We need people in our lives who have our best interests at heart but will also keep it real and tell us if our presentation was trash, or the way we treated the waiter was disrespectful, or our thinking about a situation was off. It's better for the people who love us, who hold us to high standards, to tell us the truth before someone less loving does. Sometimes those corrections can feel painful, but it's better when they're given with love.

When students or aspiring entrepreneurs come to me for advice, I feel it's my responsibility to be honest with them. If they walk out of my office not knowing what I really think, I've done them a disservice. Too often, in meetings with potential investors or connections, or even during an interview, people are given the impression that their idea is good to avoid damaging a relationship or creating an awkward moment.

There are times when people come in to pitch a new business idea and I have to tell them it's terrible. Others show up ten minutes late, acting like it isn't a big deal. Some walk into my office without having done any research on my background. Sometimes it seems like someone is just BSing me. When any of those things happen, I let them know I'm not impressed, not because I'm running my own version of *Shark Tank* but because I want them to be better prepared for the next meeting, the one that could really make or break them. The real value—the true gift—is in the input and guidance. That's why I'm often very direct. I'll tell people, "There's no way I would invest in this company, and here's why." It might not be what they want to hear, but it's what they need to hear. That honesty often leads to more work, polish, intentionality, and attention to detail that leads to better presentations, business models, job interviews, and grad school applications. And that is a beautiful thing.

My experience with Miss Johns led me to understand a key lesson: to seek and receive help when you need it. Don't wait. Too many of us think we need to figure things out on our own. Asking for help can feel like a sign of weakness, but it's not. It's a sign of intelligence to know what we don't know and to find someone who can help us know it.

I thought of this lesson recently, when I gave a talk at Morehouse College in front of eight hundred young men for their weekly Crown Forum, a speaker series where activists, scholars, and public figures of all kinds come to share their perspectives on issues like social justice, personal empowerment, entrepreneurship, and the African American experience.

I sat in a wooden chair on a stage in the King Chapel with

a professor, Dr. David Wall Rice, who was asking me questions about my life and my experiences. As I looked out at the crowd, I noticed that many of the students were on their phones, heads down, scrolling, texting, whatever. I thought to myself, *Oh man, this is not going well.* I had already lost the crowd in the first few minutes.

At that point, I decided, *You know what? Forget the format. I need to shake things up.* I shifted my whole body so that I could talk directly to the audience and asked if there were any questions. "I'm only here for fifty minutes. If you think there's something important you want to ask me, ask." Five people stood up. Just five. I was surprised. I wanted to reward them for stepping forward, for taking a chance when other people in the room would not. So I said, "For these five people who stood up, I want to buy you lunch. Unfortunately, I have to get on a plane and go to Philadelphia right after this, but what I'm going to do is give each one of you a hundred dollars."

You could feel the energy in the room shift immediately. Everyone was paying attention now. The professor interviewing me said, "Let's unpack this. Some people might say, 'Here's this capitalist coming in, flashing cash, showing off.' What do you say to that, Demond?"

I told him and the room, "Listen, the point isn't about the money. It's about the lesson. If just one person in this room sees this moment and realizes the importance of stepping up, of asking for what they need, of seizing an opportunity, then I've done my job. That's what this is about. Because if you sit back and let life pass you by, you miss out."

There are all kinds of reasons people don't ask for help:

Sometimes we are shy or too proud, or we think we know the answers. Sometimes we worry we are a bother or not worthy of help, but we have to push those feelings away and go for it. When you find someone who can help you build on your strengths, be the one who stands up. Engage. Don't be afraid to ask a question or ask for help because you never know where it might lead. Take the chance and then show your appreciation by following through and following up. And on the flip side, be a strength-finder for someone else in your life—notice what they do well, tell them what you see, and offer your support and encouragement.

What my mom did for my education—taking me out of public school and enrolling me at Inglewood Christian—single-handedly changed the trajectory of my life. Miss Johns gave me the hope and confidence to find a way out of Inglewood and to start forging a path to safety and prosperity. Turns out, I didn't need to win a McDonald's sweepstake; I could make my own luck with my own talents. The strength-finder purposefully recognizes, highlights, and helps you use your abilities to your advantage. They may actively add to your talents, as a teacher might, and like a parent encourage you not to quit, even when things are hard. A strength-finder could also be a co-worker or manager (the good kind), or they might be a friend who shows you a side of yourself you couldn't see, especially if you're being hard on yourself. These kinds of friends of the good do not let your insecurities, like mine with reading, take over; they anchor you in reality and possibility. I try to be this kind of friend of the good with my kids, a positive voice countering any doubts they might have about their paths, like my mom did for me. This is the kind of friend we all need at some point in life, and often throughout it, especially during times of transition.

Chapter 2 Insights

- Don't let a weakness define your whole story. We don't have to be good at everything—one strength can become your foundation.
- Honest feedback delivered with love is essential to growth. Correction with love isn't cruel; it prepares you for a world that won't always be gentle with its feedback.
- Don't be afraid to ask for help—it's a sign of intelligence, not weakness. Knowing what you don't know and finding someone who can teach you is how you grow.
- Be a strength-finder for someone else. Help someone identify their strengths and work through their weaknesses.

CHAPTER 3

Mo

Brother for Life

My cousin Mo is a friend of the good who is a brother for life. No one in Mo's world, or mine, lived the kind of life we envisioned for ourselves. We were anomalies. This drew us together. We dreamed of what our futures could be, and we motivated each other to reach and surpass our goals. I have other people in my life whom I trust, but some people come and go. Mo is a constant and I thank God for that.

The DJ was spinning house music, and the vibe was unlike anything I'd ever experienced. Some of the most beautiful women I'd ever seen surrounded me. Hands in the air, everyone chanted, "House music all night long!" I felt like I was in heaven. The room was engulfed in sauna-like heat, and sweat poured down my body as the energy surged through the crowd.

About a year after I moved full-time to North Carolina to

live with my dad, as soon as I got my driver's license, my cousin Mo invited me to visit him at Duke University for a taste of college life. To a kid who lived in the projects of Inglewood for three years and was now sharing a trailer with my dad, visiting Duke was like going to another country. I'd tag along with Mo to classes and parties. When I first visited, someone asked me where I was in from and I panicked. I fronted like I was a student at UCLA to impress people. Once I blurted it out, I had to stick with it, roll with it, even though it made no sense that I would be all the way across the country on a Thursday!

From my high school perspective, campus life was so relaxed and fun. But the most indelible impression of my Duke visits wasn't the parties—it was seeing so many talented, thriving Black and Brown people. Mo's circles were a different universe from mine. College wasn't a world filled with the violence and poverty I experienced in California or the racism and struggle of my small town. Back then, in the late 1980s and early 1990s, Duke was at the peak of its basketball success. Future NBA players Grant Hill and Christian Laettner were campus legends because the team was winning game after game. Mo and I got to see these guys walking around and we went to the same parties. While the percentage of Black students on campus wasn't high, Duke had the largest group of young, hard-charging, and brilliant Black folks I'd ever seen, reaching for greatness. No way I was missing out on the college experience after seeing that.

I became close to my cousin Mo because nearly every summer, while growing up in Columbus and later living in California, I went to North Carolina to stay with my Aunt

Sue and my cousins in Huntsville, about twenty miles west of Winston-Salem. I loved every second of my time there.

Driving from Columbus with my dad, I anticipated all the fun that lay at the end of the long trip when he'd drop me off. There was a welcome familiarity that came with pulling into my Aunt Sue's driveway and surveying who was on the porch to greet me—Aunt Sue, Uncle Charles, Grannie, a few cousins. Every time I arrived, I felt bathed in love and happiness.

Aunt Sue and the rest of my relatives lived in a little community on a hilltop, each of their houses next to the other. Huntsville was small as a pinhead, with a historic white clapboard Methodist church at one end and a brick Baptist church a half mile down the road at the other. There wasn't much in between. The woods came right up to the side of the road; farther on, the shoulder slid down into rich pastures and farmland.

Mo's full name is William Maurice Cowan. Mo has one older and one younger sister. Growing up, his family didn't have a lot, but they got by. His mother was a seamstress, and his father, a Vietnam veteran, was a machinist. Both graduated from segregated high schools. After my time in Inglewood, something both Mo and I could sadly relate to was being in a home where the men battled addiction and had turbulent marriages. Mo's father died in a drunk-driving accident when Mo was sixteen.

When I was in Huntsville, I spent my days riding around on the dirt bike my dad bought me and playing basketball with my cousins. Mo was the cousin I was most attached to. With Mo, I've never had to worry about being judged. When I moved back to North Carolina and even before, when I was visiting from California, Mo let me hang around with him, even though I was five years younger and always trying to show off my breakdancing moves. A lot of older kids would have said get lost, but Mo would invite me to come play basketball just like an older brother would. As we got older, the years between us shrank, but the brotherhood remained. When we were kids, Mo was pudgy with big glasses. No matter his size, he was a speed demon on the basketball court. He'd put on Rec Specs, replacing his prescription glasses, and bound all over the court. Sometimes we'd play one-on-one, but more often we'd get other cousins together for some five-on-five or join pickup games at the public courts up the road. We were inseparable.

Huntsville was the kind of place where the people on one side of the street were your family and the people on the other side of the road were related to one another. The evening activity was sitting on the porch watching what the neighbors were up to. Kids rode up and down the street on their bikes and later in cars. These were towns where you went to school, got a job working for R. J. Reynolds or in a textile or furniture factory, and eventually crossed the street to marry someone from the other side of the road. At one point Mo and I dated sisters from across the road.

Huntsville was also a town in an area where it wasn't surprising to see members of the Ku Klux Klan, in full hooded regalia, passing out literature on Main Street, near the high school, local grocery stores, and restaurants. When we played basketball together, it wasn't unusual for a pickup truck with a Confederate flag on the back to drive by and for a white face to lean out the window and yell "nigger!" at us. The Stars and

Bars planted in the middle of front lawns, the bumper stickers, the angry looks, the comments, the KKK—all of this was used to try to keep us in "our place." The intent was to maintain the social order, to prevent Black and white people from mixing, certainly to prevent Black and white kids from dating. At every turn, our families were reminded of the invisible hierarchy around us, the rigid social norms that demanded Black people should never forget where they belonged: at the bottom of the social ladder.

I can now look back at that time in my life with the knowledge of the pervasive caste system in the South, the "thingification" of Black people that Dr. Martin Luther King, Jr., spoke of, and the enduring human psyche throughout history—the desire to feel superior to someone else. In the South, particularly among poor white populations, there remained a mindset of "at least I'm not Black," a harmful way to differentiate and assert superiority. This fostered a culture of looking down on Black people, stereotyping them as unintelligent, dangerous, or criminal. Such assumptions were reinforced daily—in stores, by police officers, by teachers—constant interactions that could erode one's sense of self.

I witnessed all this firsthand. In malls, convenience stores, and dollar stores, I was often followed by employees, watched closely as if I didn't belong or couldn't afford to buy anything. It wasn't just me; I saw it happen to other Black kids too. At school, expectations for Black students were often lower, which was obvious when you looked at the makeup of AP classes—hardly any Black students were enrolled, not because of a lack of ability but because we were rarely encouraged or considered for those opportunities. I noticed, too, that there were teachers who would steer some Black students toward certain pathways, sometimes outright discouraging my friends from even applying to particular colleges, telling them, "You're not going to get in there." Instead, they'd suggest working at the local factory or other limited options, reinforcing the boundaries set by that same system of assumed inferiority.

I was lucky that by the time I moved to North Carolina full-time in ninth grade, the way I thought about myself, my place in the world, and my potential had been formed. I carried with me a deep confidence in myself. I was fortified with love from my Grannie, inspired by my dad's business, and armed with the guidance of Miss Johns. I also realized how rare it was to have a mom so focused on making sure I knew about Black achievements, something that most of my Black and Brown peers didn't have. For so many, there was always a ceiling set by parents, grandparents, great-grandparents, and the environments they grew up in. But because of Mom, I had the view that anything was possible.

My confidence was also helped by being the kind of kid who vibed with both guys and girls across different social circles. It didn't hurt that I had a 50–70 percent employee discount at Jeans West, so I always looked fresh. And my ability to get out of Inglewood taught me to move beyond fear, with purpose and determination.

But that didn't mean I knew I had a clear path to the life I wanted, one where I could make my own decisions and provide for myself and others. There was a time when my dad asked why I couldn't be more like my cousins, who were good with their hands, painting and fixing things, not afraid to get dirty. Getting dirty just wasn't my thing. My dad wanted me to have those skills because he saw them as necessary for survival, a means to make a living, but I wanted to find another path. Mo was the one who showed me that path. I needed that solidarity—not someone to push me but someone to stand with me and let me know it was okay to dream, to be different, to not squash those ideas.

In town, my Great-Uncle Buddy was the closest example of a person Mo and I could look to who seemed in control of his life and independent—that was what we wanted. No one told Uncle Buddy what to do. He decided where to show up, when, and how. Uncle Buddy owned a lot of land, but he didn't make his wealth from farming, at least not at first. He was a guy who would drive up with his truck, gun rack in the back, hand out fresh watermelon, and tell us stories about going into the woods to make illegal corn liquor to sell over the county line. Uncle Buddy was as smart as he was funny. Like any savvy businessman, he diversified, and that's when he started farming and land speculating. He was, by our measure, in a position of authority and respect, but if he had been born in a less discriminatory time, or if he had the advantage of being white, he could have been the CEO of a major corporation, making millions. Despite what could have been, Uncle Buddy's success was still motivating to me and Mo.

We knew growing up that if we stayed too long in our local community, we'd never get out. It wasn't about running away but about exploring what was possible. When I went to college, my dad said to me, "I love you, but don't come back here to live. There's nothing here for you." Mo and I acknowledged the racism we faced, and we'd encourage each other, mainly by committing to moving on when we were able to. I never felt awkward or out of place, because I had a brother in Mo, a kindred spirit who thought like me and reinforced my aspirations. Mo is brilliant, one of the smartest people I've ever known. Even as a kid I knew that—when we'd break out Trivial Pursuit, he'd know the answers to every question. But considering where we came from, Mo's acceptance to Duke was incredible. My self-esteem was reinforced by my relationship with Mo. I could dream. And so could Mo. The hierarchy that held other people back didn't apply to us. Mo and I wanted to be well-respected leaders who led by example, to build relationships, to have stable and loving families, and to not worry about paying the bills next month. We invited each other to experience whatever new chapter opened in our lives. We'd say, *Come be a part of it.*

Mo not only went to Duke but also went to law school, and eventually he became chief of staff to Massachusetts Governor Deval Patrick. In 2013, when Senator John Kerry resigned to become President Obama's secretary of state, Governor Patrick appointed Mo to Kerry's seat, and for close to six months, Mo was a member of one of the smallest and most elite groups of officials in the country: a Black U.S. senator. Mo is now chief legal counsel at Devoted Health, working to fix a broken system for Medicare-eligible people.

One of the lessons I tell my children is that your five closest friends show who you are. If you hang around drug users or heavy drinkers, or people who are cruel and mean, or people who are uncharitable, or people who cheat on their partners, you will likely adopt those same characteristics or find yourself in a bad situation. There was a guy who became a close friend in my freshman year of high school. He was one of the funniest people I knew. We spent countless hours together hanging out, cracking jokes, and trying to meet girls at the mall. We were inseparable, and I thought I knew everything about him. But unbeknownst to me, he had started selling drugs to make some extra money while living with his grandmother. One day, something went wrong with the money, and his supplier came to his grandmother's house and shot him in cold blood. He was killed right there, and the thought still haunts me—how easily I could have been there with him, playing video games, completely unaware of what was happening in his life. It's a reminder that even the choices others make can have life-altering consequences for you. But if you seek out friends of the good—people who strive and want you to strive—and if you make them a part of your life, you invite goodness into your life. Mo is an example of that goodness for me.

Mo and I are best friends, and we give the best of ourselves to each other when it comes to making major decisions—who we decided to marry, job changes, business opportunities. I call him to get his legal expertise and to break down complicated political issues. He calls me for business advice. We were the best man at each other's wedding, and we text nearly every day. It is unspoken between us that we share the good, the bad, and the struggle. People who display jealousy when you win are not friends of the good. Mo supports me not just when I am down but also when I am up, and I do the same for him.

I have always made friends easily, from grade school to high school and beyond, but I don't think I realized until later in life that many of these friendships were superficial. They were transactional or social. I was friends mostly with guys who were fun or who I could do business with but not guys I could open up to or share my fears or pain with. Women seem to have a natural inclination to share their worries and problems with one another. Men, on the other hand, can spend hours together and never really ask, How are you doing? I have spent many evenings at a game or hanging out in a bar. After being out all night, I'd come home and my wife, Kia, would ask, "How is so-and-so doing?" And I would reply, "I don't know; fine, I guess." This superficiality would surprise Kia, but it was typical for me and my friends. A lot of men keep it on the surface—a comment on the weather, a good golf shot, the news, or even a blessing in church, but never ask the deeper question "How are you, really?" There have been times in my life when I was the life of the party, but I was in pain.

I remember being in business school with a lot of folks who had a lot of money—I mean, *a lot* of money. I had no money. Big groups of my classmates would go out to dinner, fifteen to twenty guys, and we'd be laughing and talking and drinking, but by the end of the night, there'd be a pit in my stomach. I knew what was coming. Someone would say, "Why don't we play credit card roulette?" Credit card roulette was a game rich people wanted to play, where everyone threw their credit card into a hat and one card would be randomly selected to cover the entire bill, which could add up to thousands of dollars. It was one of those moments when some people's indifference about money became painfully obvious.

There was no way in hell I was going to do that. I'd have to find some way to get out of it. It reminded me that we can be surrounded by people and still feel very alone. Being able to talk to Mo about how to navigate those situations—the pain of being broke as hell while surrounded by generational wealth—was so critical. It was something he understood and helped me figure out how to deal with. He told me he had felt the same way while at Duke and assured me that it wasn't always going to be like that; in a few years my financial situation would be very different. This was just a moment in time, and everything I was working toward was on its way. Sometimes it's hard to see that clearly when you're in the middle of it.

Having someone like Mo, who has traveled the road with me and can provide honest feedback about who I am, has been invaluable. When I decided to retire from my investment career, Mo was one of the first people I talked to, after my wife. He gave me unwavering support, telling me without question that I could take this next step. He has been a rock through various family tragedies, a person I can turn to, be vulnerable with, and share moments of deep emotion. When Grannie passed away, a loss that hit me deeply, Mo was by my side, offering comfort and support.

Our shared commitment to social impact efforts has been a cornerstone of our friendship. Together, we served on the board of Roxbury Preparatory Charter School, one of the highest-performing schools in Massachusetts at the time, supporting its leadership, including John King, who later became secretary of education under President Obama. We've given advice to school leaders and mentored students. When

I need someone who can give trusted advice to my kids, and they don't want to hear it from me, I send them to "Uncle Mo," knowing he will give them wisdom about school, life, and summer jobs.

Without Mo, I don't know if I would've made it through the way I did; there certainly would have been a lot more bumps. He wasn't just my cousin, he was my peer, not necessarily in age but in mindset. I didn't need Mo to give me a bunch of advice; what I needed was that quiet reinforcement, that sense that I wasn't alone in trying to move differently in the world. Without him by my side, I might have made a whole different set of choices. That kind of friendship—brutally honest, deeply vulnerable, consistent, and unshakable—is a rare gift.

Chapter 3 Insights

- Seek out friends who see and support your highest aspirations, especially when you feel like an outlier in your environment. The right friend can reinforce your dreams when no one else understands them.
- A true brother for life is one who celebrates your successes as genuinely as their own. People who are jealous when you win are not friends of the good.
- Deep friendship requires vulnerability and honesty that goes beyond surface-level interactions. Especially for men: Cultivate relationships where you can share not just achievements but also fears and struggles.

- Your five closest friends can shape who you become. Choose those who embody the values and character you wish to develop in yourself.
- Seek out those who will travel the whole road with you, through life's transitions and challenges, providing both brutal honesty and unwavering support.

CHAPTER 4

Nick, Earl, Kevin, and Alpha Phi Alpha

Chosen Family

Nick, Earl, and Kevin were my college roommates. When I was around them and my Alpha Phi Alpha fraternity brothers, I felt like I fit in 1,000 percent. Nick, Earl, Kevin, and I shared a sense of humor, academic ambition, care and concern for one another, and a sense of style (I wasn't the only fashion maven). These guys became my chosen family, helping to reinforce who I truly was and supporting me to become the person I aspired to be. We bonded together based on mutual interests, and our connection grew deeper through common values, experiences, and service. We went through some difficult stuff, and we grew up together. When it comes to friends of the good, chosen family can be important for anyone searching for belonging, but even more so for people who may be on their own in their given family or community. Even when you have confidence in standing out, standing together with others can give you a new, powerful sense of self.

"V102! V102!"

Nick, Earl, Kevin, and I were laughing, jumping up and down, and chanting just like we did back in college. We had our arms around one another, enjoying the energy of being back at the University of North Carolina at Charlotte more than twenty years after graduation. V102 was the dorm address we shared from sophomore until senior year, and it was the place people came to hang out on campus. We had come back for homecoming and, even though it had been a while since the four of us had been together, there was no formality, no easing into it. The love immediately returned—it felt like home.

After reconnecting at homecoming, Kevin got emotional and said, "I didn't know how much I needed this." The texts have been going back and forth ever since, sharing thoughts and feelings about our friendship and many, many memories. Kevin and Earl recalled long car rides on I-85 and I-40 to go see Earl's dad when he was sick, passing the hours in deep conversation or in silence, and sometimes with laughter. Kevin remembered the intensity of realizing how vulnerable life was: "Earl's pops was one of the coolest, strongest dudes I knew. And if cancer could take him down, that was some serious shit."

Earl remembered coming back from his dad's funeral and walking into the room where Kevin and I were waiting for him. "You embraced me. You let me know I was not alone."

Nick remembered the days when his home life was less

than ideal, with his parents on the verge of divorce, and his classes stressful. One of us would wake him up to play *Madden*—he had some classic moves with a fake punt on fourth down. He said the relaxation of being together, laughing until we were crying, was the best therapy. And he talked about what it meant to see other people like him pursuing a degree in business and accounting and graduating. "I come from a family of educators," he said. "There was no example for me in the business world. You guys didn't know it, but you were my examples to follow." For Nick, the feeling he got from us was similar to what I felt with Mo as someone charting a life different from his family's. It's a comfort to be in the presence of people doing what you are trying to do.

When I left home for college in 1992, I went on my own. No one drove me, helped set up my room, or put sheets on my bed. It wasn't that my family wasn't supportive—they encouraged me—but they couldn't get time off from work or afford to be there in the same way I saw other kids' families were. They also didn't know things that could help me, like how to pick the best dorm and meal plan or find a work-study job. Going to college alone wasn't that different from the way my life had been. I had always been somewhat on my own, in either a literal or a symbolic sense. There were people in my community who wanted to go to college, but often it was the local community college. They were thinking about how to survive—paying the rent, taking care of kids, or just getting to next week. I was thinking about all of that, too, but also about how to be a leader, how to move beyond the boundaries of my circumstances. Other than Mo, there weren't a lot of people in my circles thinking in that way.

Until I went to college, met my roommates, and joined a fraternity, I didn't have much of a community of like-minded folks. I lived with my mom and dad while I was in high school, and I was popular, making people laugh and getting good grades, but other than Mo, I wasn't really close to anyone. Those passing relationships in high school were often transactional or filled with surface-level conversations, more like friends of utility or friends of pleasure. I wasn't worried about going to parties or playing sports as much as other kids my age. I was more focused on the future. Seeing Uncle Buddy as a successful businessman and the independence my dad had with his tow truck business led me down a path where my drive for college and career success made me feel different from everyone else. And then I went to UNCC.

When I arrived on campus, it was like coming out of the wilderness. Twenty-five percent of the student population was Black—suddenly, all around me there were Black folks, Black culture, and comfort in being an intellectual among other intellectuals. I found myself surrounded by kids who cared about academic progress. We talked about regular stuff like basketball and video games, but folks were also talking about their professional ambitions, about wanting to be doctors and lawyers and business leaders. There was a connection on every level: shared ambitions, shared music, shared sense of humor. It was a space with a ton of cool, funny, smart people, and it was like they were telling me, *Hey, come join us. You belong here.*

I got to know Nick, Earl, and Kevin in freshman year. The three of them went to the same high school in Durham but weren't particularly close until UNCC. There was a lot of cracking on one another and "your mama" jokes. But it wasn't just that: These guys were so brilliant and quick-witted that anytime you walked into a room, no matter if we were playing spades or video games or just sitting around, you had to be ready because your clothes, your hair, your shoes, the person you were dating were all fair game. For those who don't know, this was the "dozens," a battle of wits. Developing my verbal skills by being around these guys was like sparring in a boxing group for four years and then realizing I actually knew how to fight.

Starting sophomore year, we moved in together. We lived in four single rooms connected by a living room and kitchen in a building everyone called Smurf Village, named for its blue paint. From then on, we shared a living space, academic hurdles, a social life, and an inner life. We were all basically away from home for the first time.

Nick and I were both accounting majors. Accounting courses can be tedious and increasingly difficult each year. We would have to analyze companies, balance sheets, and income statements looking for the smallest mistakes. We had to build spreadsheets and crunch data. We studied for every major test together, staying up until two or three o'clock in the morning. We would drink Mountain Dew to stay awake, reviewing materials, sharing notes, quizzing each other, and filling in any gaps. If I'd been on my own, I would've gone to bed two hours earlier, but we kept each other sharp, encouraged critical thinking, and stayed in it together.

V102 wasn't just about homework and studying. We

stayed up late playing Sega Genesis, talking, laughing, and having fun. We listened to a lot of music together; Earl introduced me to John Coltrane. We began to learn how to actually cook, which, in the early days, was treacherous. My first attempt at fried chicken resulted in me slathering barbecue sauce on some raw chicken and putting it into a hot skillet—pure disaster! This was also the time when several of us started dating the women we would eventually marry.

An early mentor of mine on campus was Derrick Griffith, God rest his soul. He was student body president. He saw how much I wanted to engage with others and encouraged me to get involved in student government when I was a freshman. One of my first projects involved working to address campus safety. Women on campus had concerns about feeling unsafe walking through wooded or poorly lit areas. I took those conversations to the vice chancellor of student affairs, advocated for emergency phones to be installed across campus, and worked to secure funding. It was like a course in negotiation—meeting with people, persuading them, and figuring out how to allocate resources.

By sophomore year, I decided to run for student body president. Convincing the entire university that I was a worthy candidate required a robust campaign strategy. I even persuaded a senior, a longtime campus leader, Lisa Odom, to be my running mate. We chose the slogan "Experience That Counts," which was a valuable lesson for me. I recognized what I didn't have—three or four years of experience on campus—and leaned on her strengths to build a full, balanced team. That's something I still do today: I never pretend to know or have everything. I surround myself with the right people.

Student government was an extraordinary training ground for me, a place to learn how to navigate systems and institutions. I created the first version of a shuttle service to help students get around campus and the surrounding areas. Students desperately needed it, whether to get to work-study jobs, make it to class on time, or even just go grocery shopping. I had to present my plan at city hall to advocate for funding and turned it into a project for the university.

Student government also gave me exposure to leadership at the highest levels. I became close with Chuck Lynch, the vice chancellor of student affairs, and attended dinners at the home of Chancellor Jim Woodward, who became a profound mentor. My interactions with these men and the guests they were hosting opened my eyes to a world of opportunities I hadn't seen before. I built relationships that would be valuable for the rest of my life.

And in the midst of all that growth and change, Nick, Earl, Kevin, and I had one another's backs. They showed up for me in ways no one else ever had. When I spoke on campus, they were there, rooting for me. When I ran for student body president, they handed out pamphlets and asked people if they had voted yet. There were so many times we acted as a shield for one another physically, mentally, and spiritually. We were all juggling so much—joining organizations, managing demanding academic programs, stepping up as student leaders. We'd push ourselves to the point of exhaustion, but we stayed protective of one another, making sure no one hit their breaking point. When we were joining our respective fraternities, people would sometimes come looking for one of us, expecting him to complete some task like going to get late-night food or doing someone's laundry. We'd cover for our roommate—"Oh, he's not here" or "I haven't seen him"—even if he was hiding out in the next room, catching a break.

I knew I wanted to join a fraternity. I saw right away that a lot of the great parties were hosted by fraternities, but it wasn't just that. Black fraternities and sororities, known as the "Divine Nine," have played a unique role in college life and in history. The oldest Black fraternity, Alpha Phi Alpha, was founded in 1906 at Cornell University. Fraternities were formed as a place of safety and refuge and connectivity; the great parties came later. Until the 1950s and 1960s, Black students were often excluded from community life and activities on college campuses, including white fraternities, athletics, student government, professional organizations, even facilities such as libraries and dining halls. Black fraternities were also a source of catalytic change in the world, pivotal through every moment of consequence in the civil rights movement.

Alpha Phi Alpha organized campaigns, protests, and voter registration, and played a significant role in Martin Luther King, Jr.'s 1963 March on Washington for Jobs and Freedom. Alpha Phi Alpha also led initiatives like "Go to High School, Go to College," promoting education in the African American community. The Delta Sigma Theta sorority organized the National Library Project in 1937 to deliver books to rural Black communities and continued to support education with the Delta Research and Educational Foundation. Rosa Parks, a member of Alpha Kappa Alpha, refused to give up her seat on a segregated bus, an act of bravery that led to the Montgomery bus boycott of 1955–56. Omega Psi Phi participated in sit-ins and protests in the 1960s, and one of its members, Benjamin Hooks, went on to become the executive director of the NAACP from 1977 to 1992, working to advance civil rights legislation, combat racial discrimination, and increase minority voter participation.[1] Many of our great leaders were and are members of these organizations, including poet and activist Langston Hughes, Supreme Court Justice Thurgood Marshall, Congresswoman Shirley Chisholm, congressman and civil rights leader John Lewis, Vice President Kamala Harris, and TIAA CEO Thasunda Brown Duckett. This legacy of service and leadership was a big reason I wanted to join.

Even though Nick, Earl, Kevin, and I were tight, my roommates and I went our separate ways—Nick and Earl went for Omega Psi Phi, aka Ques, also known to be a little bit "off the chain." Kevin became a member of Kappa Alpha Psi, where the "pretty boys" hung out. And I knew I wanted to be in Alpha Phi Alpha, the fraternity of Martin Luther King, Jr.

We didn't have a house; most Black fraternities didn't have the money for that. But we did a ton of community service projects: mentoring kids, cleaning highways, and raising money for schools and homeless shelters by running a car wash or selling doughnuts.

Another of our fraternity's shared projects was prepping for step shows. We spent months practicing in secret for competitions, grueling rehearsals of disparate individuals working together to perform and often win. A few days after I was revealed as an Alpha, we went to the biggest event I had ever participated in, my first step show. There were a bunch of teams and thousands in the audience.

The precision, the clapping of hands, the stomping, the yelling—"Ice, Ice, Baby! Too cold, too cold!" Hearing the crowd yell, "Goooooo, Demond!!!!"—it was incredible. There was a moment that set the crowd on fire: We formed a three-level pyramid to a slow R&B song and collectively gave a sexy thrust to the crowd. The stadium went nuts. I had never felt anything like that before.

Fraternity brothers and Alpha Kappa Alpha sisters had come from all over the state to cheer us on. Nick, Kevin, and Earl were there too. I was the first of the four of us to join a fraternity, even though we all had that aspiration. They were cheering their heads off for me, losing their minds. It wasn't about a particular frat; it was the whole Black community showing up at the step show, celebrating together.

All of that practice—falling, trying to get the pyramid to work, nailing the precision of every move, the timing—I was doing it with my brothers. That practice, that work, that time together built lifelong bonds. And then to win together? That stamps a connection. But even the losses didn't matter; we were together, pulling for one another.

We also spent hours and hours planning parties to show off our moves, laugh, and celebrate our joy. Most of those epic nights happened in the Lucas Room, which was always packed and full of energy. Lucas was a big activity space in the Cone University Center, back when the student union was there. From ten at night to one in the morning, hip-hop and R&B had the whole crowd moving. A student who went by DJ Will One smoothly mixed the songs to make the crowd jump—tracks like Method Man and Mary J. Blige's "You're All I Need to Get By," Mobb Deep's "Shook Ones," OutKast, the Fugees, and so much more. The sweat, the bumping and grinding, the stepping—it was nonstop. Those Lucas Room parties were always hot, and the energy was unmatched!

When building a fraternity brotherhood, we focused on finding well-rounded individuals who embodied the values we wanted to represent. There were people who were super charismatic and fun, friends of pleasure. Then there were people who could have boosted the chapter GPA, friends of utility. But we were looking for something deeper. A strong fraternity is about more than just parties or achievements—it's about creating a brotherhood that brings both joy and substance to its members. If members aren't invested in the bigger picture or in supporting their brothers, they aren't people you can rely on when it really matters. It isn't about finding perfect people or aiming for sainthood but about building a group with a shared moral compass. Too often, the values piece is what's missing. We wanted brothers who you could party with at night and count on to show up for a service project the next morning. Those are the relationships that create the strongest bonds in a fraternity.

Community service has always been deeply personal for me. Serving people has never been a theoretical exercise. There have been moments when I've seen my grandmother, my cousins, and my neighbors in the faces of the people I'm helping. When I serve, I see the possibility of myself in their circumstances—it's not abstract or distant. When I work with programs like the Martin Scholars, I see kids without resources, without capital or the know-how to navigate systems. Regardless of whether they're Black, white, or Asian, I see their struggles, their obstacles, and the injustice of it all, especially given the talent they possess. I've been there, and I want to help. That connective tissue to my own life is why it feels so urgent.

A fraternity brother of mine, Ty, told me that his children know and understand the power of our brotherhood and what it means to him. "Our combined energy and love are palpable. Anyone who spends time around it feels it. My children feel it and know it. They have been hearing your names all of their lives." Now his son has joined Alpha Phi Alpha, and he said he feels like it is an opportunity for a lifetime of love and support that is trickling down to the next generation. My fraternity was a new chosen family for me at UNCC, providing another home base and teaching me about brotherhood, service, and leadership.

At UNCC, first my roommates and then my fraternity brothers taught me that the powerful force of good their camaraderie and community provided could be diluted by friendships with people who fell short. I've learned the hard way that relationships that harm your virtue, diminish your happiness, or hold you back from success can literally or figuratively lead to your downfall. Sometimes you can spot these "bad actors" through the smallest things, like seeing someone toss trash on the ground when they think nobody's looking, or how they talk down to a salesclerk or waiter, as if that person doesn't matter or isn't worthy of respect. I've had friends who would talk about money nonstop, and after a while, it made me start thinking about money all the time too. Keeping negative or selfish friends close is like having a terrible soundtrack playing in your head. Their bad habits start to become your bad habits. Their flaws start to become your flaws.

In order to really know what friendship is, you have to see what it isn't first. I've encountered plenty of examples of what friendship is not. There are jealous people who can't celebrate your wins. If I ever catch myself dampening who I am, hiding my spirit, talents, personality, or intelligence—that's a huge red flag. And if someone isn't dependable, or if I hesitate to be vulnerable with them, then I know I can't trust them to support me when it matters. I don't want to call out specific folks because that's not my thing, but I learned my lessons. Thirty years after college, the signals are the same.

In college, I knew I could do it all—study hard and still enjoy myself—but it required balance. There were always distractions. People would ask, "Why are you studying? Let's go to the day party," or try to pull me away the night before an exam, so I put disciplines in place to stay focused. And I made it a point to spend my time with people who supported me, who knew what was important to me. Whether it was my roommates or my line brothers or others, they'd say, "Yo, D is not going," and back me up.

When you get older, you don't often go out all night with a group of friends and then head to Waffle House when the sun is rising. You don't often work on service projects where you spend all day together and then bunk up at night. On campus we invested in one another, we checked in, we had each other's backs. We were vulnerable; even when we were broke or scared, we didn't feel like we had to pretend, we would just talk it out. There wasn't one big moment that turned my roommates and fraternity brothers into my chosen family. It was a series of small moments strung together to build a bond that has lasted to this day, and that's why we could show up to homecoming after twenty years and feel the memories and the love come flooding right back. Our common interests drew us together and made us feel like we belonged, but our common values kept us together. It was easy to be with these people, and it still is.

A study done in 2005, called the Australian Longitudinal Study of Ageing, found that close relationships with children and other relatives have little impact on how long a person lives, but people with the most friends tend to outlive those with the fewest by more than 20 percent.[2] Family is super important to me, but we can't choose our families, and sometimes the families we are born into make life more complicated or challenging. Friendships, especially when we choose well, can help create the kind of family we might need.

I found my original chosen family at UNCC, but none of this has to happen on a college campus. In the United States, as of 2022, a little under 40 percent of adults had a bachelor's degree.[3] A chosen family can be found in other places and at other stages in life—in the military, on a community service project team, or in a volunteer program. You can also find a chosen family at a job where you realize you aren't the only person who loves to code for hours in the dark and watch anime to relax. A job with a common mission like fighting climate change or poverty is another possibility, or join a church choir, a running club, or a travel group. If you seek out people who want to pursue a shared interest or passion, and if you have similar values and work together, I think you'll quickly find a chosen family you can count on. You can build trust and understanding and a different kind of home, one that you chose and that nurtures you. Being fortunate enough to recognize the people who truly have your back and to share life with them is one of the greatest blessings you can experience. It's a gift I deeply want for my children and my nieces and nephews because I know that kind of friendship provides a foundation I can never fully give them. I'm starting to see this unfold as my kids choose their friends. Kia and I have talked with them about it a lot, and they've also grown up seeing the people in our lives who aren't blood relatives but are still called "auntie" and "uncle." Observing those relationships has given them a blueprint for the kind of friends they want to surround themselves with. It's beautiful to see how those connections are shaping their own understanding of loyalty, trust, and love.

Some of us grow up feeling like we don't belong in our own families or towns or communities. Some are the "onlys" at school—the only Black student, the only queer kid, the only one who loves art or West Coast rap. Walking out and into a bigger, broader world and finding a tribe of like-minded people can, for some, be the first time they have ever felt like they belong. Acceptance and belonging are so essential to happiness—I have seen that in myself and my kids.

In many ways, these two groups of people—my roommates and my fraternity—set the standard for what it means to have friends of the good. Through my leadership roles in student government and with my fraternity, my identity and sense of purpose were further shaped. The things we accomplished together reinforced this belief: I have the ability to make a difference in people's lives and so I should. This is what I'm supposed to be doing. Countless experiences of service, leadership, and fun showed me what a chosen family should feel like.

Kevin, Earl, Nick, and my brothers from Alpha Phi Alpha—our lives haven't always been as intertwined as they could have been, but coming back together on campus, I saw immediately how much connective tissue remains. Watching them go from being college kids to becoming fathers and mentors and leaders, and staying connected, the ease with which we still roll, the immense love we feel—this is a chosen family in which I belong, every time.

Chapter 4 Insights

- Chosen family provides a sense of belonging that reinforces who you truly are and supports you to become the person you can be. Seek out people who accept you 1,000 percent.
- Show up, especially when it matters.
- Opening ourselves to vulnerability with those we trust transforms friendships into deeper, more meaningful bonds.
- Build connections through common interests and common values, and strengthen them through shared experiences and service to others.
- Chosen families can be found in many contexts

beyond college—through service, work, faith communities, or shared passions. Actively seek out these connections throughout life.

- The bonds of chosen family can provide lifelong support and friendship that studies show contribute significantly to health, happiness, and longevity. Invest in these relationships.

CHAPTER 5

Erskine

Second Father

> There is no doubt Erskine Bowles, my boss at the White House, changed my life, but not just because of the opportunities he made available to me. Over the three decades I have known him, he has been more than a mentor or sponsor: He has invested his time, energy, and reputation in me. He is a friend of the good because he was an advocate for me as a professional and as a person. Someone in Erskine's position has the power to open many doors, provide experience, and share wisdom, and that's meaningful, but he went beyond all that: He brought me into his world. He is like a second father.

"Come work for me and I'll change your life," Erskine Bowles said to me in August 1997, the summer after my senior year in college. I had been working as an intern for Vice President

Al Gore's team out of the Eisenhower Executive Office Building, just to the west of the White House. As the program came to an end, I was recommended for a permanent position working for Erskine, who was chief of staff to the president of the United States. My interest was piqued. How could it not be? I knew this opportunity was not something I could pass up.

But staying at the White House after the summer ended was a serious change of direction for me. I had planned to return to my job at Arthur Andersen, a top accounting firm at the time, where I had worked since sophomore year. I got the job through a program called INROADS. INROADS provided opportunities for first-generation as well as Black and Brown college kids to work in corporate settings while in school. The program also had classes on résumé writing, business dinner etiquette, and interview prep. These are the basics for landing a job in the corporate world, but many of us haven't had those experiences or someone to guide us through the specifics. It's not that complicated, but when you don't know, you don't know. Without access to this information, the cycle of excluding Black, Brown, and first-gen students from getting office or corporate jobs continues. INROADS was trying to make sure that experience and knowledge were available and that the cycles of exclusion could be broken.

INROADS organized campus visits where company representatives explained what they were about and interviewed potential candidates. On interview day in my freshman year, I was sitting in the auditorium next to the head of INROADS's Charlotte office. When Arthur Andersen came up to present, she leaned over and said to me, "That's the company that pays the most." That got my attention. I didn't have any money, and when I graduated, I would have no money *and* college loans to pay off. At the time, "pays the most" was the best metric I had. Later I would learn that chasing money is a terrible way to evaluate an opportunity, but back then it just seemed like the surest path to financial independence. So, without a second thought, I replied, "Well, that's the company I want to work for."

A week later, I had a fantastic interview with the senior manager, Russ Charlton. "There's just one issue," he told me. "You're a finance major and we only accept accounting majors." I was fast on my feet and responded without missing a beat: "Funny you should mention that. I was just about to change my major." That was enough for Russ. I was hired. Throughout college, I worked at Arthur Andersen, and they offered me a full-time job after graduation, which seemed like the most reliable opportunity I had ever had—a stable, consistent, attainable career that would help me support my family.

Working at the White House, even for a summer, was not part of my original plan. But sometime during my final year at UNCC I went to a reception for another former student body president, Karen Popp, who had returned to campus for a speech. After UNCC, she went to law school, joined a prominent law firm, and clerked for a federal judge. After a stint as a federal prosecutor in New York, she became associate White House counsel in Bill Clinton's administration.

One of my mentors, Chuck Lynch, the vice chancellor of student affairs, introduced us at the reception. We ended up chatting for a while. Her experience in the administration intrigued me. I had never met anyone who worked in the White House or even in politics. I was fully intending to make ten thousand dollars that summer at Arthur Andersen, which seemed like a fortune, but by then I wasn't just thinking about money. I didn't expect to leave the event contemplating an unpaid summer internship, but the White House was definitely different. "You know, I already have a job after college, but I'm wondering if there's anything I can do for the summer at the White House?" I asked her. "Sure, kid, send me your résumé," she told me (and yeah, she really did call me "kid").

The White House summer internship program application window had closed, and even though I had just met Karen, she still did whatever it took to get me in. I must have made a good impression, but she made those moves for me because Chuck Lynch and Chancellor Jim Woodward gave her my background and their endorsement. As student body president, I had built up a reputation with these two men. Having that leadership position on campus, responding to them with respect, showing my intense preparation, delivering when they needed me to was like a multiyear interview. So, when the time came, they vouched for me. And that was enough for Karen. It's amazing what the support of a few friends of the good can do.

Most of the interns at the White House were political science majors, so my accounting focus made me an anomaly. Unsure of what to do with me, they assigned me to work for Vice President Al Gore's finance manager, building spreadsheets and helping with budgets.

Now crunching numbers might not sound exciting, but I

spent the summer loving everything about the White House. I loved the quiet in the morning before the tempo picked up to a pace that I imagine is unmatched anywhere else on the planet. I loved being in the place where decision-makers from the president down through every layer of leadership debated, planned, and decided how to run the most powerful nation in the world. Every day was something new. The work was not difficult for me, but I was walking through hallowed halls of greatness. There were ceremonial aspects of the environment, like photo ops and the Easter egg hunt celebration, but at the end of the day there was real work that had to be done to keep the country running smoothly.

When I was working as a summer intern, I didn't know that a full-time position was even a possibility, but I still tried to squeeze every last drop out of the experience, so I busted my butt. I didn't go out and party with the other interns, or take the time after 5 P.M. to explore D.C. This was an unpaid internship, but I approached it in the same way I did everything else, and I didn't leave until I had done everything I could to help. And that seriousness made me stand out. I built a reputation for being organized, responsible, and reliable. I also kept in touch with Karen Popp, making sure she knew how much I appreciated what she did for me. I am sure my work ethic and follow-up were why someone suggested I consider a position working for Erskine. And that's how I ended up with multiple interviews all the way up the West Wing food chain, until the only person I hadn't yet met was Erskine himself.

The day of the interview with Erskine is carved into my memory. I crossed the street from the Eisenhower Building to the White House, excited about what was possible. The building was quiet and pristine. The West Wing is much smaller than people would think, just a handful of offices of people who meet with the president regularly—during my time there, people like Vice President Al Gore, future Supreme Court Justice Elena Kagan, and Senior Advisor to the President for Policy and Strategy Rahm Emanuel.

When I arrived, the Marine on duty was at attention, and an escort walked me to the chief of staff's suite, just off the Oval Office—it was intimidating. But as soon as I stepped into Erskine's office, there was an instant connection.

I've been in rooms where people are sizing you up, trying to decide if you belong, but with him, I knew immediately that I did. The warmth of his handshake, his direct eye contact, and the way he carried himself put me at ease right away. He wasn't formal or stiff. He was kind and thoughtful. Erskine welcomed me in his soft North Carolina accent and invited me to sit down.

Within minutes, he told me, "Demond, I've heard a lot about you, and I'm impressed." Erskine was lean and tall, with a narrow face and owlish glasses. I had seen him on TV and in the newspapers many times during my internship, but this was my first time seeing him in person.

Since I had already met with everyone else on his team, his questions were about my family and about going to UNCC. A lot of leaders think they need to make employees fear them, or that they need to test you. He didn't interrogate me, or try to trip me up. I still would have taken the job if he'd done all that. Instead, he made me feel like I didn't have to prove myself, even though I was fresh out of college and had only ever been an intern. He just said, "I want you here." He showed me who he really was, and that only made me want to work for him more. That's great leadership.

It was a short interview and soon after I started working for Erskine. Far away from the number crunchers, it was my job to answer phones, make copies, take notes, and escort senators, heads of state, and celebrities to wherever they needed to go. I would join Erskine for events and lead him through crowds, although at least once I got lost—that didn't go over well. Erskine was kind and generous, always, but that didn't mean his standards weren't high.

Every morning, I had to prepare for Erskine's arrival, so I was usually the first member of the West Wing staff to show up. I would collect daily briefing materials that were prepared for him including top secret clearance materials, newspaper clippings, and memos that helped prep him for meetings he had that day. All of this would go on his desk.

I also answered the phone and kept up with voicemail. Some people's voices became familiar to me because they called frequently to ask for favors or to lobby for issues and things they wanted done. I was able to do a very good impersonation of Jesse Jackson. He would always start off the call by saying, "Hello, this is the Reverend Jesse Jackson. Is Erskine in?" Those moments are seared into my mind because many of them were so surreal. The people I saw on television and in the newspapers were a part of my daily life.

I was sometimes one of the last to leave too. Everyone employed full-time at the White House stayed until their own boss went home, whether that was at 6 P.M. or midnight. You had to, because if you slacked, a thousand eager and talented people were waiting right outside the door to replace you. We all believed that the work was so extraordinarily important. The thing that drove us was not the fear of being fired, as it would be in many jobs; instead, we were driven by the greater good.

At Arthur Andersen I had worked in the auditing group, analyzing companies and testing the validity and accuracy of data. In the White House, my job was more tactical and sometimes menial, but I was proximate to brilliance, to extraordinary people doing the impossible, regularly, and some of that rubs off on you. We were trying to make the country stronger financially by balancing the budget; to make healthcare more affordable and accessible; to help people feed their families—this was all part of a higher calling, certainly more inspiring than auditing financial statements at an accounting firm.

During my internship I stayed in Alexandria, Virginia, sleeping on my fraternity brother Shawn's couch. Every morning, I drove my Geo Prizm across the Potomac River and circled through Washington, D.C.'s quiet downtown streets until I reached the West Wing entrance. I would flash my blue badge, the most coveted entry pass in the White House, and the Secret Service agent on duty would wave me through the gates. That feeling, going through those gates—it was so cool. At the end of the day, I'd do the trip in reverse. A few times, I would drive home, shower and change my clothes, and turn right around to go back to work without sleep.

My dad got me the Prizm after my green Honda hatchback broke down during my senior year in high school. I was so proud of that car because it was in reasonable shape. But one day, as I was headed back to Shawn's, my Prizm began coughing blue smoke. It wasn't a little tailpipe exhaust—smoke billowed out from under the hood. I somehow managed to get the car back to Shawn's. I don't know much about cars, even though my father is a mechanic and owns a tow truck company, but I knew enough to realize that it was a wrap. After I got to work the next morning, paying for a very expensive taxi ride, I told everyone what happened. I wasn't trying to get sympathy; I wanted to disclose the situation in case it somehow interfered with my duties. It wasn't an option to be late to work at the White House.

Erskine got wind of my car trouble, most likely from his secretary or someone else on the staff. He probably didn't know the details of my living situation, but he did know that I didn't have a lot of financial resources. He figured that I was in a difficult spot and wanted to help. That's the kind of person he is, always trying to problem-solve. We had worked together for about five or six months, so he knew I was reliable and consistent. Later that same day, on his way through the open space outside his office where my desk was, he asked me another life-changing question: "Demond, why don't you come live in my house? I have a spare room. You won't need your car. I am living in a mansion by myself."

My first reaction was, "Oh, no, sir. I'll figure it out." And then as quickly as I said it, I realized I didn't have any other options and the price was right. I couldn't pay for a taxi every day or get an apartment closer to downtown. And it could be pretty amazing to spend that kind of time with Erskine. I reconsidered and accepted his offer.

Every morning, sometimes as early as five-thirty or six o'clock, a Secret Service agent drove us to the White House in a Lincoln Town Car. We bonded during that time. Sometimes he'd read the paper; sometimes we would chat or talk business. I remember pitching him a wild idea about putting free-standing gas tanks in various convenient locations to make it easier to fill up. It was a terrible idea, but he listened and complimented at least one aspect of it that was important in my consumer success stories—location, location, location. Because Erskine trusted my desire to learn, he let me sit in on meetings with leaders like Secretary of State Madeleine Albright and Treasury Secretary Robert Rubin. I rode on Air Force One with President Clinton. But Erskine and I also hung out, had dinner many nights, and watched football together. One weekend, his Uncle Rich came to visit. He told joke after joke. I can't ever remember laughing that hard. It was in those moments that it started to feel like family. This experience of being with Erskine was so different from living in North Carolina, where Black and white, rich and poor, were separated. I began to tell him my life story, and he told me his. On the surface, there probably couldn't have been two people less alike: a Black kid who grew up poor and a white millionaire many times over who helped elect a president and became one of the most powerful people in the country. But we also had a lot in common: the struggles with family and pain of loss and the found humanity between the two of us.

In the typical work environments of corporate America, we often focus on the things that make us different—our status in the organization, our education, our cultural backgrounds, our gender—and what we miss are all the things we have in common. I never would have become so close with Erskine if I hadn't accepted his offer and taken that chance. I'm not suggesting that this is the kind of thing most people can or should do—it was a very unusual circumstance; I literally had nowhere to live—but if we hadn't lived together, I never would have gotten to know him the way I did. That's how the relationship moved from mentor to something deeper: second father.

The list of concrete ways Erskine has helped me is immense. Because my time with him overlapped with scandals, tobacco litigation, and the balancing of the budget, I learned about the inner workings of crises and major negotiations. Every day I saw how seemingly simple things could actually be more complicated than they appeared to be on the surface. And then I figured out how to navigate those situations. A meeting, for example, seems simple—figure out who should attend and when they should be there. But when you are dealing with incredibly busy, important people with a myriad of competing priorities, that simple task can get complicated quickly. I remember when a committee head was late because he was finishing up a calculation, and Erskine was sitting in his office with Secretary Albright, waiting for six people to come in. It was an absolute disaster to keep the secretary of state waiting, and that was embarrassing for Erskine.

In a high-pressure environment, I learned to distinguish what was an emergency from what was not. In the White House, everything seemed urgent, but when you are juggling the news of a nuclear arms scare with a constant barrage of people who think their issue is the most important one, you learn to stay calm and clearheaded and prioritize. I remember the panic I felt the first time I got a call from President Clinton for Erskine, which I thought would be a priority over anything else. I immediately ran down the stairs to a bathroom on the lower level. I called to Erskine over the door of a stall, disrupting his quiet time. It turned out nothing was more important than that.

The experience of being in the White House and interacting with high-profile congresspeople, U.S. secretaries, and CEOs taught me something else—I was no longer impressed or intimidated by meeting anyone. That level of comfort was a gift as I progressed through the rest of my career.

I also learned about myself. After I joined his staff, Erskine would tell me, "You know, Demond, you have some of the best people skills of anyone I've ever met." This was coming from a guy who had helped Bill Clinton get elected. It was a huge compliment, and he said it over and over. I was flattered, but after a while, it started to bug me. "What about my other skills?" I finally blurted out one day. That was when he gave me one of the toughest and single most valuable pieces of advice I've ever gotten.

"You lean on your people skills really hard. You need to balance those people skills with technical expertise. And when you do that, you'll be unstoppable."

That piece of advice made me think of a basketball player who could only dribble and shoot with his right hand. He might make every basket, but only being good with one hand, he's never going to make it to a Division 1 college basketball team, let alone the NBA. But if he could go left or right, he'd be unstoppable. I was in danger of being that right-handed basketball player. If I wanted to succeed and be truly outstanding, I needed to be able to use both my hands.

At first, the advice made me defensive, but it turned out to be exactly the feedback I needed. I was using what came naturally to me, but I was leaning on it too hard, not doing the work to learn what I did not know how to do. Erskine encouraged me to develop analytical abilities and skills. That simple exchange drove me to become fanatical about learning every technical aspect of whatever topic I studied, whether it was a White House policy issue or an investment decision down the road. That lesson—to learn to dribble with my left hand—from my friend of the good became the engine of everything I do to this day.

Erskine changed my life by giving me the best of himself. He wanted my experience working at the White House to add up to more than an impressive line on my résumé, but that required a different level of engagement from him. When my car broke down, it was hardly his responsibility to help me figure it out. And I am sure I would have, but maybe that would have meant less sleep and missed workdays; I would not have been able to perform at my best. He took me in. When I fell short in my technical skills, Erskine could have thanked me for what I did well and sent me on my way, but he didn't. He took the time to figure out how he could help me do better, giving me some of the most important advice of my career. As I walked out the door, Erskine could have handed me a letter of recommendation, which would have had tremendous value, but he did more than that. He encouraged me to take the GMAT, then wrote me a recommendation for

Harvard Business School and about twenty letters of introduction to investment firms after I got my MBA.

When someone would ask Erskine who I was or do a reference check, he wouldn't say "Demond is a good guy" or "Demond is smart and hardworking." He would say I was his son. He let everyone—businesspeople, U.S. senators, governors—know that they should treat me as they would treat his white son. People would repeat it back to me all the time. Erskine would tell someone how important I was to him—my success and who I am as a person. He did things for me that a father would do to support his children: He tried to protect me, worked to create opportunities for me, even put his own reputation on the line for my sake. That's so different from just having a mentor. A mentor might write you a letter of recommendation, but Erskine would pick up the phone and personally tell someone how much I meant to him, how I'd made a difference in his life. That's not just doing a favor; that's trust, the kind of trust where you'd let someone live in your house. It's a whole different relationship.

His level of confidence in me, his respect for what I brought to the table, was always clear. He noticed things, he paid attention, and he genuinely cared. To this day, he is like a second father to me, and yes, he still calls me son. We share life's joys and pain: when a loved one was sick, when I tore my Achilles, when he was dealing with back pain. We'd call each other up, tell jokes, and talk about our families. And when he ran for the Senate, I was right there knocking on doors for him, doing anything he asked.

One of my proudest moments was bringing my dad to the White House, having him walk into the West Wing—my father meeting my second father. He sat down across from Erskine, and Erskine told him what an incredible job I was doing, how I was a significant contributor to the team, and how much I was helping his office and the country. My dad didn't have the words to respond; I could see he was overwhelmed by being in the White House and then hearing Erskine talk about me.

Afterward, I walked my dad throughout our workspace and out of the office. When I came back in, I stepped away for a moment into the bathroom and cried. I was so overwhelmed with pride. To have my dad, who introduced me to hard work, hear those words about my impact on one of the country's highest offices, and to know deep down they were true . . . it was everything. It became further motivation for me, but not to become a politician. Going into my internship, after being student body president, I thought perhaps I would run for office someday. After seeing the scrutiny and destruction of people's lives from the intensity of the public eye and media, I knew politics was not for me. I would take everything I learned and move on to the next adventure.

Erskine invested in me in a way that was about structurally changing my life. This kind of friend of the good is rare, I know that, but it's important to recognize them, even if you just catch a glimpse. Someone who does more than open a door for you. Someone who makes an extra investment in how your life might turn out. When that happens, go through that door and then work as hard as you can to prove that the extra investment was worth it.

It is up to those of us farther along in our careers to look for ways to help young people that go beyond giving advice or providing a connection or even a scholarship. That's all valuable, but every once in a while invite someone into your world and into your life. We must aspire to give as much as we have received. Give someone the best of you, and you will have made a friend of the good for life.

Chapter 5 Insights

- Learn to dribble with your left hand. Use what comes naturally to you but work on the skills you're missing.
- The best opportunities available to you are often not in your plan.
- A true advocate invests in you beyond opening doors; they invest their time, energy, and reputation to structurally change your life path.
- Accept honest feedback that challenges you. The most valuable guidance often identifies your blind spots, not just affirms your strengths.
- Proximity to greatness, even in support roles, teaches invaluable lessons. Being in environments of excellence allows some of that brilliance to rub off on you.
- When someone offers extraordinary support, work hard to prove that their investment is worthwhile. The relationship requires reciprocal commitment.

CHAPTER 6

Kia

Ride or Die

Kia, my wife of close to thirty years, is the most incredible and most important friend of the good in my life—she's my ride or die. I could have built a life and then asked someone to join that journey, but instead I married someone I could build a life with. Without Kia's push, without her encouragement and spiritual grounding, many of my life's most critical decisions would have been completely different. She provides the perfect balance to my "run hard until it gets done, let's save the world, anything is possible" approach. Marriage is a relationship you can't step away from; you must show up every day. Through our three decades together, Kia has been beside me in my most difficult moments and shared my happiest ones, and I've tried to be there for hers. Who you marry influences everything: your career path, your family choices, how you spend your leisure time, your community contributions, your deepest dreams, and even your health. Kia hasn't just shared my world—she helped create it by making me better in every choice along the way.

In my sophomore year at the University of North Carolina at Charlotte, I found myself in the middle of a brawl. For weeks, secret practices had been under way in preparation for a ceremony featuring a step show and a big reveal. Over the course of the event the crowd went wild. It was rowdy and fun and uplifting, but someone somewhere in this group of around five hundred spectators must have bumped into someone else and egos puffed. Suddenly people were pushing and fighting. I tried to be a peacemaker, stepping between people to keep them from swinging at one another, but the fight quickly escalated.

Little did I know that as I was trying to calm people down and break things up, someone was about to rush me from behind. As the guy approached, ready to deliver his sucker punch, my girlfriend Kia clocked the guy on the head with a cane, stopping him in his tracks. Kia was a church girl, not much of a fighter. The only other fight she had ever been in was with another girl in middle school, and the other girl did all the fighting. But in that moment, she had my back. I looked at her in amazement, and I thought to myself, *This is the woman I'm going to marry.*

Kia and I met early in my sophomore year, through a UNCC initiative called the University Transition Opportunities Program (UTOP) set up to bring incoming students from underrepresented communities to campus for six weeks during the summer before their freshman year.

It is a program intended to help students find their footing and their confidence before being thrown into the chaos of the first year of college. UTOP was run by a man named Dr. Herman Thomas, whom we called Doc, a professor at UNCC and a trusted adviser to the university's chancellors. While I was attending a two-day visitation for accepted students, Doc stopped me in a crowded student center and convinced me to sign up. It's worth digressing for a minute to talk about Doc, who is another friend of the good. He was like a coach who, in this case, prepped students for the big game of college life.

Doc had a whole history of helping Black and Brown people, stretching back decades into the heat of the 1960s civil rights struggle. In the 1950s, he attended what is now North Carolina Agricultural and Technical State University and was arrested in 1956 when he and other students tried, unsuccessfully, to desegregate the Swain County school system. Four years later, he took part in organizing the first student lunch counter sit-in on February 1, 1960, in Greensboro. Four students from North Carolina A&T sat down at a Woolworth's counter and refused to leave. Doc wasn't one of those four students, but he helped coordinate the protest, which was a seminal moment in civil rights history. Later, he became a champion of helping to uplift students like me.

Because I followed Doc's advice to go through UTOP, I started school with a tight group of friends, including Nick and Earl, a supportive network of professors and UNCC staff, knowledge of the various offices that were useful, like financial aid, and seven credits toward my graduation, all before officially matriculating. Those credits were crucial and made it possible for me to run for and then win the election for student body president in my sophomore year.

In my second year at UNCC, I became a counselor for UTOP, and I modeled myself after Doc. He had a way of empowering young people by delegating responsibilities, allowing us to make mistakes, and encouraging us to keep growing. Even though the students were just a year younger than me, I was in a position of leadership, counseling and advising forty to fifty kids. That experience helped me grow as a leader on campus and left a lasting impact on who I am today. When the new students arrived, I was there to meet them and get them situated on campus, just as someone had done for me a year earlier. And that's how I met my future wife.

Kia was one of many eager new faces, although I didn't really notice her at first. Not too far into the program, the students began organizing themselves for a UTOP talent show, an annual tradition. We were in the common area of Hawthorn Hall. I was at the back, watching as the show participants stood one by one to practice.

I clearly remember when Kia stood up in her floral-patterned dress, opened her mouth, and began to sing. I swear in that moment the heavens opened, and divine light burst over her as she began a gospel song. Everything stopped and everyone fell silent, listening to her exquisite voice polished from years of church choir. That's when I started paying attention.

A few weeks later, Kia mentioned that her math grades weren't great, and I, as her mentor, concluded that the reason must be all the time she was spending with her off-campus boyfriend instead of studying—an obvious distraction. I suggested she get focused and break up with her boyfriend. The way she tells it, she immediately went downstairs to the pay phone, called him, and ended their relationship. Kia was a first-generation college student in a completely new environment. I was there as an adviser, along with a couple of others and Doc, and presented myself as someone she could turn to for guidance and insight. Her goal was to do well. And I was put in a position to be helpful. I genuinely wanted to help, but to be clear, I was also eliminating the competition. Conveniently, I was available to be her math tutor. And, you know, it all worked out.

About a year into dating, Kia and I were walking through the mall when we stopped at a jewelry store. She wandered over to the engagement rings. I watched her, already knowing she was the woman I wanted to marry. She browsed the display cases, looking and looking, her eyes suddenly sparkling when she saw one particular ring. A huge smile spread across her face as she grabbed my hand and pulled me over to the glass.

"Look at this ring," she said. "It's so beautiful. If we ever get married, it would be amazing to have this ring. Oh my God, it's perfect!"

The ring was called Juliette. It was stunning, but at the time, it was far out of my price range. But I didn't forget about it, and thanks to my accounting job over the summers and various work-study gigs, I was able to save up enough money over the next three years to buy the very ring she had pointed out that day.

Kia and I dated for four years before I proposed. Several of our friends, even a few who had dated for less time, got engaged before we did. One of my fraternity brothers proposed to one of Kia's sorority sisters after only a year or two of dating. He did it boldly, at one of the campus shows, and the buzz spread quickly. I could sense Kia's growing frustration, but I had a plan.

After I graduated, while Kia was still in her junior year, I bought the engagement ring and booked a getaway to Cancún, Mexico. It was our first time traveling internationally, and I couldn't have been more excited, or nervous, about the surprise proposal I had in store.

When we arrived at the Cancún airport, my nerves went into overdrive. There was a random security process where, after passing through the gate, if the red light flashed, your luggage would be opened and searched piece by piece. My heart was racing. I had the ring in my suitcase, and if I had to open my bag in front of Kia, it would be obvious what was going on and my plan would be ruined. Fortunately, as I stepped up to the security stand, I got a green light and walked through.

When the time came, I asked Kia to take a walk with me. Once we reached the perfect spot, I grabbed her hand and asked her to pray with me. I had the ring in my pocket and my heart was pounding. As we prayed, I asked God to bless us. I told her how much I loved her. While her eyes were still closed, I dropped to one knee. When we finished the prayer, I said something like "You are the woman that God has placed on this earth for me to love, and I want you to be my wife."

Kia opened her eyes—and fainted. Literally fainted. Luckily, I had the presence of mind to catch her. Some of the people nearby had been watching me get down on one knee, and then they saw her collapse into my arms. We both ended up on the sand as I held her. She opened her eyes, screamed, "Yes! Yes! Yes! I'll be your wife!," and started crying. The people around us were clapping. There was so much joy. It was an incredible moment, one I'll never forget.

We planned to get married a year later, after I was finished with my job at the White House, meaning we'd be apart for more than a year of our engagement, only seeing each other once a month. A lot of girlfriends or boyfriends might have pushed back or given their partner a hard time about leaving, but she supported me wholeheartedly.

It was a tough year. When it was time to visit, I'd take Greyhound buses or fly on Eastwind Airlines, which had a big bumblebee painted on the side of the plane. The buses were bad, but the flights were worse, constantly delayed. A flight scheduled for 4 P.M. could easily turn into a wait until 11 P.M., with no one around to explain anything. It was exhausting, but through all of it Kia stayed supportive because she recognized this was an extraordinary opportunity for me—and for the life we were building together.

After I finished working for Erskine at the White House, I headed back to North Carolina, back to my job at Arthur Andersen, ready to marry my college sweetheart, which I did on June 13, 1998, outdoors at Tanglewood Park in Clemmons.

Kia had just graduated from college, and I was only a year and a half out, so many of our college friends were in the wedding party—I think we had about twelve groomsmen and bridesmaids. When we took the pictures, we had to use a panoramic lens to capture everyone! Mo was my best man. Grannie and my parents were there too. All the men wore tuxedos, though mine was a little big, and the women were in dresses with stockings, traditional church fashion. Everyone looked beautiful, but it happened to be at least a hundred degrees in the North Carolina sun that day. People were baking and sweating. Mo said it was the hottest day of his entire life. We didn't have a backup plan for the ceremony—if it had rained, we would have just been out there in the rain.

The wedding was incredibly important to our family. Like many people, we ended up spending way too much on it. But the family pitched in, buying flowers and even getting discounts on the cake, photos, and more. When we stepped out and were introduced as husband and wife, the band played "Unforgettable," the duet version sung by Nat King Cole and his daughter Natalie Cole. It turned out to be the perfect song because it captured how I feel about Kia so well. She is unforgettable, amazing, and has made my life so much better than it ever would have been without her.

We went on a honeymoon to Bermuda, thanks to Erskine, and then moved in with my dad in his trailer, living with him for a few weeks before I started at Arthur Andersen and our lease in Charlotte began. Then I had to decide what to do with the rest of my life. Arthur Andersen had seemed all right to me when I worked there during college, but when I went back, after spending time on a daily basis with senators, heads of state, CEOs, and civil rights activists in the White House, I felt that a career in auditing wasn't going to be my life. I wanted something bigger. I asked to be transferred to the consulting division and that was better, for a while. Kia and I talked about other possibilities—me going to business school, her getting a graduate degree. It wasn't an exact plan, but we were constantly strategizing, dreaming, and supporting each other. After working seven days a week for more than a year, I needed to clear my head, and she was the person I talked to the most about what the future might look like. It was a good thing I changed course too. Arthur Andersen, which was the largest and most prestigious accounting firm during its time, was eventually caught up in the Enron scandal and collapsed in the early 2000s.

When I was younger, before college, I thought that I would have to get my life right—a career path, a steady income, a home—before getting married. It would be nice to figure it all out and then settle down, but the truth is, if you marry the right person, they will help you make tough decisions, and you will build a great life *together* as opposed to building a life and then bringing somebody in.

Sometimes being a ride or die means taking an interest in the other person's world. A few months into our marriage, when Kia was teaching fourth grade in Charlotte and I was working at Arthur Andersen, we had a little misunderstanding. She'd come home completely exhausted, and I'd think to myself but wouldn't say out loud, *You think you're tired? You have no idea what tired really is. My job is exhausting!* I honestly thought her job was easy, but my view of things was way off. I had no clue what a teacher actually did, all the planning, the grading, the behavior management, and extra responsibilities teachers carry.

I started to learn more about Kia's world when she asked me to take part in the Junior Achievement program at her school, teaching the kids some basic concepts about money and economics. No big deal, right?

My first time was a complete bomb. I went in there and used a lot of business terms, only slightly dumbing it down for nine-year-olds. I didn't have any gimmicks and didn't know the first thing about teaching. The kids were squirming all around while I stood there sweating, completely lost. I could see I wasn't connecting—just blank stares looking back at me. Meanwhile, Kia sat in the corner, with a smirk on her face.

I left school that day and had to take a nap, I was so tired. When I woke up, Kia was like, "You see how hard it is now?" That hit me. Here I was, thinking her job was easy, and I couldn't keep a classroom engaged for even an hour.

I'm supercompetitive, so the next week I showed up prepared. I bought a bunch of candy as incentives, created games, and set up competitions around questions. *That* changed the whole flow. It became a really fun class, and the kids began to look forward to me coming. I started looking forward to it too. This experience changed our marriage. I went from initially dismissing Kia's exhaustion to understanding it firsthand.

I began to have a better appreciation of what her days were like, and it brought us closer together. Sometimes you just have to experience something to really get it. It's hard to describe what it's like to be an investor to someone who's never done it, just like I couldn't understand teaching until I tried it. Kia did the same for me. While she did not come into the office and do financial analysis, she actively engaged in my world, particularly in the early days, getting to know my business partners and attending events. I tried to shield my family from the ups and downs of the stock market, but otherwise we were in it together. We created this reinforcing mechanism of investing in each other, strengthening our bond and our relationship. That's what ride or die is about.

That doesn't mean our marriage is perfect. We have very different personality types. I wake up joyful at five-thirty in the morning, like, *Hey, how you doing? What's going on?* And I'm an extrovert. When I don't get the same kind of enthusiasm and energy back, it can be frustrating. Kia is an introvert. She needs time to recharge, especially in the morning! Some things you don't notice until you get married. When you are dating, you're trying to make a good impression, so you might not roll out all your specific qualities. We learned more about each other over time, and how to talk about things together, especially through our church's marriage ministry (more on that in chapter 10).

Another important lesson I've learned is how to give love in the way Kia wants to receive it, even if it's not necessarily how I want to receive it. Physical touch and words of affirmation are the ways I feel loved, but quality time is how Kia, and my kids, want to receive love. I didn't understand that at first, and I still have to be reminded of it.

At some point, a few years ago, I asked Kia to say the words "Demond, you are *great*." This might sound crazy to some, and initially it certainly did to Kia. I have seen marriages destroyed when people I know looked for validation elsewhere because they needed someone to appreciate them. When the road gets bumpy, it can be tempting to look outside your marriage for fulfillment, validation, or a bit of baggage-free distraction, whether physical or emotional. It's easy to focus too much on the mess, the struggle, the organizational puzzle that is marriage and then along comes someone—a neighbor, a co-worker, a person at the airport bar—who says, *Hey, you're great! You look good. You're smart*. It's normal and natural to be attracted or excited about someone new, someone who doesn't know you forgot to pick up the kids, doesn't know about the plate left by the sink and not in the dishwasher, and hasn't seen your face, the same face, day in and day out for years. But taking our frustrations and desires outside of our marriage will make us more and more indifferent to it. If there is always an option to get love and support elsewhere, you won't do the work to build that at home. Kia and I have always been each other's first and best adviser, hype man/woman, and source of support.

Love starts as magic, a spark, but what draws people together may in fact be the opposite of what keeps people together—successful marriages don't happen magically. Getting married means making a promise, exchanging vows and rings and kisses before God and family, but the maintenance of those bonds is a lot of work. Life inherently brings hardship, struggle, and sorrow. You and your ride-or-die spouse have to be able to work on tough issues, discuss and debate, find a happy medium, and laugh even when you experience pain. Your spouse should be consistent, dependable, and share the same values. I noticed Kia because she was beautiful, talented, and a natural leader. But it was her character that made me realize she was the woman I was going to marry. A person's character lasts, and hers is extraordinary.

When my sister, Tonia, was diagnosed with cancer at age forty, she had a husband and three kids. Kia had supported me through loss—when my grandmother and Uncle Buddy died—but this was different. By the time Tonia was diagnosed, it was too late to save her, the result of a lack of preventative care. My brother-in-law was doing everything he could—he's an extraordinary human and loved my sister with all his heart—and my Aunt Sue would often be there to support Tonia as well. I was right there with everyone too. I went to nearly every treatment and appointment with Tonia, and the whole experience was emotionally draining. I'd stay up late to talk and laugh with her, play gospel music, sometimes even sing in my terrible voice. In front of my sister, I'd try to keep her spirits up, but as soon as I walked out of the room, I'd be weeping.

During all of this, I was working through the ups and downs of the stock market. Meanwhile, we had small kids, and Kia took care of nearly everything on her own—caring for them when they were sick; cooking dinner; driving them to school—while working as a professor, allowing me to grieve. Coming home from a trip to see Tonia or from a long day at the office, I was completely drained, emotionally, physically, and mentally. I'd have nothing left to give. Even though I was happy to be with my family, I was thankful that Kia didn't ask to hand things off to me or say, "Your turn with the kids."

After Tonia passed away in 2013, I carried that grief. There were moments when I'd start crying out of nowhere. I didn't fully understand the value of therapy back then, so I tried to deal with it internally. I was struggling to keep it together emotionally, to help my nephews and my niece and maintain my position at work. Thank God Kia was my best friend. She listened to my pain, held me while I cried, gave me space when I needed it, and never complained when I had to catch up on work to stay excellent at my job.

This is what our partnership has always been. A marriage of more than two decades isn't about some perfect, equal split of responsibilities. People think it's 50/50, but sometimes it's 60/40, or 90/10, or even 130/-30. People go through cycles, and sometimes one person needs more from the other and then it reverses.

Kia shows up. That sense of showing up for others was ingrained in her from early in her life. When she was in a beauty pageant or a singing competition, fifteen extra people would show up to support her—church aunties, family, friends. She came to college on the first day with three carloads of people. Showing up is one of her defining characteristics. No one I've ever met has had that same unwavering loyalty. In times of joy and in times of crisis, that quality has been exactly what I've needed. If you're Kia's friend, you never have to question whether she'll be there for you. Anyone Kia calls a friend can depend on her 100 percent.

I have always been a person who shows up for my friends, but before I met Kia, I was someone who operated in small groups or alone. The idea of consistently showing up for a wide circle of people wasn't natural to me. But through Kia, I witnessed something I realized I wanted for myself—the ability to be present for all those moments others might write off as small or insignificant but that actually matter. When Tonia passed away, an entire group came to rural Kansas for her funeral. When I saw all those incredible people show up, I cried and cried. It bonded me to everyone who attended. I did not expect them to come, but I was so glad they did. Their sacrifice said something profound about our relationship.

I remember when a new colleague at Adage lost his father, just a few weeks into the job. A handful of us traveled to another state and stood in the rain during the service. It would have been perfectly acceptable not to go to that funeral. It was not easy to get there. We had just met, so there were no expectations, and we were all busy with the stock market, but I'll never forget the look on his face when he saw us there. I told him, "We are family. This is what we do. We show up." That's what Kia taught me.

My relationship with Kia has so many dimensions and connections, and in so many ways Kia makes my life better. When we faced problems that seemed difficult for us to solve, we sought and engaged in professional help. Sometimes you just get stuck, and you need a skillful third party to point out where that stuck-ness is and how to work through it constructively. But the one thing that Kia and I have always said, even in our toughest moments, is that we love each other; we'll put in the effort and figure things out. Our love is stronger now than it was when we got married, even after everything we've lived through. Kia and I could fill a hundred bathtubs with the tears we've shed together over the years, and we've busted up laughing a thousand times. She is as much a friend of the good to me today as she was when she clocked that guy over the head with a cane.

Chapter 6 Insights

- Choose someone who will have your back in crisis.
- Character outlasts all other qualities. Beauty and talent might catch your attention, but integrity, dependability, and shared values sustain a partnership across decades.
- Marriage isn't fifty-fifty; it shifts with life's seasons as you take turns carrying each other through challenges and grief.
- Step into each other's worlds to build understanding. Experience your partner's challenges firsthand rather than dismissing what you don't understand.
- Provide the validation your partner needs. Tell them they are great and pay attention to their best qualities. Give them the affirmation they seek so they won't look for it elsewhere.
- Your natural way of showing love may not match how your partner needs to receive it. Learn each other's love languages.
- Be best friends, not just partners. Share tears, laughter, and everything in between.

CHAPTER 7

David and Jim

Guiding Lights

David and Jim, both professors I met at Harvard Business School, are friends of the good who are guiding lights. When the world kept trying to tell me what I wanted wasn't possible, they showed me the way to greatness. Early in life, my vision was limited to people like Uncle Buddy. As I grew older, I might have seen a Black lawyer in town. Later, I added accountant, corporate executive, university president, and business owner to the list of possibilities. But then I met Jim and David, who were Black men operating at the highest levels of the corporate and academic worlds with excellence. These friends of the good lit the way, giving me confidence, comfort, and a new foundation for how far my vision could expand.

There was a day back in 1996, during my summer internship at Arthur Andersen, when my manager, Russ Charlton, came into my office and said, "Hey, would you like to go to Harvard?" I wasn't sure if he was serious. He told me Harvard Business School had a summer program for potential MBA candidates from low-income or underrepresented communities. "Absolutely," I said without hesitation.

"Great," he said and walked out of the room.

After he left, I thought to myself, *Where the fuck is Harvard?*

I learned Harvard is in Cambridge, Massachusetts, when I shipped off to the Summer Venture in Management Program. It lasted less than a week. The participants were mostly—if not entirely—Black and Brown college students.

I was sitting in a classroom when a professor, Jim Cash, walked in to teach. He was a giant, six feet six inches, with a wide smile and gentle eyes. When he opened his mouth to speak, his voice was soft, smooth, and kind. And unlike any other professor who had stood at the lectern before us, he was Black.

For an hour he talked, and I listened, absolutely riveted. It wasn't just his lecture on a beer manufacturer that held my attention but the tales of his incredible success. In 1965, Jim was the first Black scholarship athlete at Texas Christian University. He played on the freshman basketball team (freshmen were not allowed to play varsity in those years), competing in places that had not yet seen Black athletes. A year later, he integrated the varsity team while being subjected to racial slurs and prohibited from staying in certain hotels with the rest of his team. By 1967, a lot had changed, and he became a standout college basketball player who would later be honored alongside Kareem Abdul-Jabbar and other top collegiate players. After college, Jim earned a master's degree in computer science and a doctorate in management information systems from Purdue University. He joined the Harvard Business School faculty in 1976 and became the first Black tenured professor. He was also on the boards of Microsoft, Walmart, and General Electric. I had never met a Black man like Jim before.

After his class finished, I skipped my next lecture and chased Jim down the street to a taxi stand, where he was waiting to leave. We talked for forty-five minutes. When he asked about my background, I told him about my upbringing and said that I wanted to do something incredible with my life. I vowed to return to Harvard Business School as a student. I came home from that experience with high hopes and excitement about Jim and Harvard. I had bought a T-shirt that I told myself I would not wear until the day I was admitted to HBS.

But I almost didn't make it.

In the fall of 1998, I applied and was accepted to the business schools of the University of Michigan and Columbia. I was awarded scholarships at both. Harvard Business School had fallen off my list. Fear held me back. When society throws out so many messages that you don't belong in certain places, that you aren't good enough, it starts to get to you. *You're not good enough* says the voice in the heads of people of color, women, and anyone else outside the "norm." So instead of embracing what could be an extraordinary next step up, you just sort of take yourself out of it. No one can reject you or turn you down if you don't show up. And that's what I was about to do.

I told Kia I was going to Columbia, a very prestigious

school and Erskine's alma mater. But she said, "Are you kidding me? What have you been thinking about, dreaming about, the last few years, ever since you stepped foot on the Harvard campus, and now you're not going to apply? You're crazy." That was the kick in the butt I needed at exactly the right time. I barely finished my application by the deadline. I was applying in the third and final round, and I worked on it until the very last moment, literally running to the FedEx office thirty minutes before it closed. If Kia hadn't pushed me, so much of what happened in my life afterward would not have happened at all or would have been very different. Thank God for Kia showing up and having my back, again.

Soon after arriving at HBS, I met my second guiding light, David Thomas. A brilliant brother from Kansas City, Missouri, David taught a business administration class called LEAD, which focused on leadership and organization behavior. David has a sunny round face, a big grin, and the build and stance of a prizefighter. When he walked into the classroom to teach, he would turn his jacket inside out and fold it into a neat square and then engage his whole body in the act of teaching, sweating through his shirt by the end of class. He was the kind of professor who didn't accept BS answers, but he was also warm and made the people around him, whether a full classroom or a single student, feel like they mattered. He maneuvered through the world with swagger. I wanted to get to know him, but it wasn't until an encounter with the police that I pushed myself through his office door.

On the night of the encounter, in the spring of 2000, I was

looking sharp—black pants, a maroon dress shirt, and a checkered blazer—on my way home from an event hosted by the McKinsey consulting firm. As I was getting off the Harvard shuttle, two officers approached me and said, "You fit the description of someone that robbed a Starbucks at knifepoint. Can you please step to the side?"

At the time, I was six months into Harvard Business School, ID in my pocket. My résumé included being the former assistant to the White House chief of staff with top secret clearance. I had been in rooms with CEOs and heads of state and flown on Air Force One with the president of the United States. But in the eyes of a few Cambridge police officers, I was just another nigger. I was detained on a sidewalk by the police because somewhere in Cambridge, a Black man had committed a robbery.

I felt I was moments away from being arrested. *Stay calm,* I thought at the time, *let it play out*. I told the officers that I had a cellphone in my pocket, not a weapon. I knew not to make any sudden moves.

More police arrived. A half dozen officers scattered themselves around me, each with one hand close to the grip of their gun. After a while, one of the officers told me that the victim was in a nearby cruiser, and they wanted me to do a perp walk next to the car. More time went by. The officer came back. The woman had changed her mind. "She's too afraid to try to identify you," the officer told me. "You can go."

I heard a description of the assailant crackle over one of the officers' radios: A "Black man in a red T-shirt," the voice said.

A red T-shirt.

The only thing I had in common with the assailant was that I was Black. Because of my skin color I was automatically a suspect. And because I was Black, the woman who was robbed was afraid to even look at me through the window of a police cruiser.

The hour of pent-up rage and fear spilled out of me. "You motherfuckers," I shouted at the police. "You kept me here all this time, and I don't even fit the description. You held me for an hour based on the word of a white woman who didn't describe anything other than the color of my skin. You just rounded up any Black man who was nearby. Give me your badge numbers!" The officers hustled to their cruisers, and the cars pulled away, leaving me alone on the sidewalk.

That night was not my first experience with racism. When I lived in the projects in Inglewood, California, I remember running to the store, just an excited kid going to buy a candy bar, and having an officer stick his head out of his patrol car, yelling, "Where are you fucking going?" I was pulled over with friends in North Carolina after dark, and when the officer shined his flashlight into the back of the car and I asked if everything was okay, he shouted, "Shut your fucking mouth." My friends were thrown up against the wall for no reason.

Until the 2014 death of Michael Brown in Ferguson, Missouri, there was little data about police stops, their outcomes, and the impact on Black and Brown communities.[1] Now we know more, but even with new data, new tracking, and new programs to try to combat racism in policing, the names of Black people killed by police keep rolling across our news feeds: Eric Garner, Tamir Rice, Freddie Gray, Alton Sterling,

Philando Castile, Botham Jean, Atatiana Jefferson, George Floyd, Breonna Taylor, Daunte Wright.

Almost every Black person in America, at some point in their lives, has had a traumatic encounter with police. A simple gesture, movement, or word, or a misinterpreted look, could lead to a confrontation that results in injury or death. There is no upside to making your well-articulated argument to a police officer. When you're alone on the side of the road, any rage or anger needs to be hidden and pushed down, no matter how you might feel. Police officers are supposed to protect people, but for much of history, especially in certain geographies, police have been complicit in the subjugation of Black people in the United States. Some police have played a role in perpetuating the longest running marketing campaign in American history: skin color as a determinant of intelligence, criminal behavior, and work ethic. The list of achievements on my résumé most often means I am accepted by others in elite spaces, but as you go down the career and education ladder, that campaign is more likely to succeed. Not every encounter with the police goes badly for people of color, and not every police officer is racist, but on this night, I was dealing with the consequences of bias and discrimination.

In David's office, he sat there, listening to me intently, asking thoughtful questions about who I was and the journey that led me to business school. In those hours, he wasn't just my professor—he was a Black man who truly understood the weight I was carrying. This wasn't something he had just seen on TV; he had lived it. He shared his own journey of growing up in Kansas City, attending elite institutions, and learning how to navigate the many challenges of racism. He had experienced exactly what I was going through, and more. He had figured out how to maneuver these environments in ways I hadn't yet, and his insight was invaluable.

David listened and responded soberly, but not without emotion. "Look, what do you want to do?" he asked me. "Because we can go after every single one of those officers and put what happened on full display." David was all in. He didn't tell me what to do; he told me about negative interactions he'd had with police, how he'd handled them, and then let me make a decision, knowing that I had his support either way.

After talking for a long time, I eventually decided that I didn't want that experience to define me or my graduate years. I didn't want to use my time, energy, and money to hire lawyers and then to be the subject of an article in *The Boston Globe* or the *Cambridge Chronicle* that would force me into the public eye.

Until that night on the street corner, I believed that being at Harvard would lift me above the day-to-day confrontations and judgments that come with being Black in America. I believed there was such a thing as "making it," a level of achievement that could take you beyond being seen as a threat. I thought there was a degree of success that could place you above the stereotypes perpetuated by the marketing campaign. It turned out I was wrong; the psychology behind that campaign is so deeply ingrained that such a place doesn't currently exist. Harvard wasn't a shield from racism. With this realization, I could have withdrawn into despair, and the incident could easily have derailed my MBA studies.

David's calm and generous guidance is what stopped me from spiraling into anger and frustration. Instead, I could focus on what inspired me at Harvard, including new mentors like David and Jim.

David was recruited to come to Harvard by Jim Cash and considered him a mentor, as I did. We are hardly alone. Many students, professors, deans, CEOs, and tech leaders have said, "You know, Jim Cash is my mentor." Starting with his push for me to apply to HBS, Jim has given me advice throughout the time I have known him, including where to send my kids to school and what boards to join. Because our offices are in the same building now, I often pop in to talk to him. He always sits back and listens, then gives direct advice. I remember when I was asked to join the board of a big public company, and I was weighing the decision. "Now why would you want to do that?" he asked me. He helped me evaluate the situation, and he explained what his process would be if he was making the decision. He has shown me what is possible, he has seen what I have done, and he knows what I want to do, so he is always pushing me to level up.

Jim told me about his experiences being the only Black man in boardrooms and conference rooms, learning to navigate spaces that Black people have rarely had access to. It was an element of business that no class could have taught me, that no seminar could have illuminated. And when I eventually moved into those boardrooms myself, having Jim to talk to and strategize with was an incredible asset. A number of my closest friends are older than me by ten years or more. As a result, they've given me wisdom and insight into how to function in places that historically have been reserved for white people. Without their counsel, I believe I would have been much less successful.

After I graduated from business school, Jim invited David and me to play golf at his club, and we were both terrible. I was in every sand trap, and it was a little embarrassing. But that didn't matter. That's the thing about golf: It gives you real, uninterrupted time with someone, just walking (or riding in a golf cart) and talking about life. In the business world, you might be lucky to get thirty minutes on Zoom with a person you admire, but a round of golf can turn into six hours of honest conversation. That's the equivalent of twelve thirty-minute meetings. It would be impossible to get twelve meetings in five years with someone of that caliber. There's simply no other setting where you get that much quality time to really connect, share stories, and build trust. And that's what David and I did, year after year, and still do.

What I learned during those hours was not about the game. David gave me some of the most important advice of my career. He taught me how to navigate spaces where I was often the only Black person in the room. He told me why it was crucial to speak up and make sure my value is recognized. He'd seen those rooms before—consulting for top investment banks, advising CEOs, teaching executive programs at Harvard—and he never seemed intimidated. From him, I learned to trust my instincts, have confidence in my perspective, and step forward instead of waiting for permission. That insight helped me find my voice and claim my place at the table.

Jim guided me through my decision to leave the hedge fund Adage and found WellWithAll, where he is now the lead independent director. I knew leaving Adage and starting WellWithAll was exactly what I was supposed to be doing, but the fear of leaving what is certain, particularly financial stability, for something less certain is very difficult. In the start-up world you don't know who is going to pay for your health insurance, or if you are even going to be able to raise money. According to Crunchbase, only 1 percent of venture capital backing goes to Black-owned businesses. And within that tiny percentage, even fewer raise more than $1 million, and I definitely wanted to raise more than $1 million.[2] I had taken calculated risks before: leaving my mom in Inglewood to go to school back in North Carolina and choosing the White House over my job at Arthur Andersen. I had confidence in my plan, but having it reinforced and supported by Jim made a huge difference, for me and for Kia. He said, "Look at the evidence; you can do this."

Jim has influenced and inspired me in so many other ways too. He is a trustee of Massachusetts General Hospital and suggested that I join the board of a hospital myself. I try to return the favor by showing up for him. When Texas Christian University dedicated a statue to Jim, I was there to cheer him on. He's asked me to be on a number of boards and committees, like the Bert King Foundation scholarship committee at Harvard Business School, and also to mentor students who are interested in finance. Anything he's ever asked me to do, I do.

Those experiences expanded my own networks. Working

together with other board members deepened some existing friendships and created new ones. When I was on the HBS H. Naylor Fitzhugh scholarship committee, I was a mentor to Kwame Owusu-Kesse, who went on to become the CEO of the Harlem Children's Zone. Kwame is someone I talk to regularly about issues of health equity and how to scale nonprofit work. He was a mentee to whom I gave advice and insight, and now he is a peer and doing the same for me.

I don't think I could have imagined my career at Adage and the path beyond without David and Jim investing in me, which inspired me to find a way to light the path for others. Almost a decade ago, I decided to contribute to a project that was just kicking off called Embrace Boston, a memorial to Coretta Scott King and Martin Luther King, Jr., unveiled in 2023 on Boston Common. Made of bronze, the sculpture of their intertwined arms is twenty-five feet wide and twenty feet tall. It was inspired by a 1964 photograph of the Kings embracing after Martin received the Nobel Peace Prize. *The Embrace* was designed by the artist Hank Willis Thomas and MASS Design Group. It is meant to be a symbol of unity, love, and shared commitment to equality.

While Massachusetts is often thought of as a progressive state and has a history in the abolitionist movement, it also has a past of intense racial turmoil and discrimination. Paul English, a Boston tech entrepreneur, came up with the idea to put this sculpture in Boston Common to symbolize a new Boston. The reality is, since I moved here in 1999, a lot has changed, and I want Black people to see that symbol and feel comfort and their own potential. Embrace Boston, thriving under the leadership of Dr. Imari Paris Jeffries, is now a guiding light for those who don't have a David or Jim in their lives.

My friendship with both Jim and David goes both ways. When a relationship begins with one person acting as a role model or mentor, sometimes the mentee thinks they have little to offer, but often that's not the case. Things change, age compresses with time, and mentees discover that they in fact have contributions to make now or in the future. Asking a mentor like David or Jim, "What can you do for me?" gets old. A better question is, "Is there anything I can do for you?" Giving back to a mentor, even in small ways, makes a difference. It may seem like someone at a high level of achievement doesn't need anything, but everyone needs help with something. Even if it's just a prayer or a kind word or letting them know, *Your advice, guidance, or support really helped me.* Being a mentor can be heavy, and sometimes being a leader can be lonely, so having someone say they are thinking about you can be a gift.

I have reached out to younger people in my life many times for wisdom: to ask how social media is changing commerce, what trends are hot in apparel, and what they are doing with AI. I want to understand what's interesting or important to their generation, and I hope I always feel there are people who can be helpful to my growth in some way. No amount of wisdom or experience means you don't have a lot to learn. Being a guiding light is about sharing your wisdom, experience, and time to help another person recognize something in themself that they did not see.

Chapter 7 Insights

- Representation transforms what you believe is possible. Seeing someone who looks like you succeeding at the highest levels provides a new foundation for how far your vision can expand.
- Guiding lights believe in your potential before you fully see it yourself. They push you past self-doubt and help you take risks that align with your true capabilities.
- The right mentors share wisdom about navigating spaces you've never entered. They provide insights that can't be taught in a classroom about pursuing dreams that feel like uncharted territory.
- Support during major transitions is invaluable. When you are facing decisions with significant uncertainty, guiding lights provide both reassurance and realistic assessment of your abilities.
- Mentorship can evolve into friendship over time. Relationships can become more reciprocal, with both parties offering value and wisdom to each other.
- Pay forward what you've received. When you've benefited from others lighting your path, find ways to illuminate possibilities for those coming behind you.

CHAPTER 8

Phill

Catalyst

Phill Gross did something that no one else in the investment world would do for me: He gave me a shot. He knew that newly hired people in his firm don't come in brilliant; they become brilliant by spending ten years with brilliant investors. Investment firms give golden tickets to the people they hire, and those tickets have often not gone to the talented top African American MBA students graduating from Harvard Business School, or Stanford, or Wharton. That's hundreds of graduates a year in those programs alone who could be creating generational wealth for their families. Instead, they're passed over because they're not "the right fit." Phill gave that ticket to me. As a friend of the good, he stewarded my education as an investor again and again. My knowledge, experience, and success compounded year after year until I was no longer his mentee but his partner.

After George Floyd's murder in 2020, my phone began ringing. I was a senior partner at Adage Capital, a hedge fund based in Boston. Many organizations, under pressure from investors, began taking a hard look at their racial diversity, and that included investment funds and hedge funds. Twenty years prior, I had applied for jobs at some of the very companies that were now calling for advice. I had applied with a Harvard Business School pedigree and recommendations from White House Chief of Staff Erskine Bowles and Microsoft board member Jim Cash, but I never got an offer. I was not "the right fit."

Twenty years after they rejected me as a job candidate, they complained that they couldn't find talented Black and Brown people to hire to change the complexion and diversity of their workforce and management teams. I had an answer for them, but it was something they didn't want to hear: *I am sure I was not the only applicant you interviewed who didn't meet your "expectations," and I seem to have done okay. So maybe the problem isn't the candidates; it's your process.*

When I started at Harvard in 1999, my plan for what I would do after graduation was vague. Like many people in my class, I took a summer internship in tech. I worked at a software company outside of D.C. that I was very excited about. This was a time when a ton of people were becoming rich, on paper at least, working at software and internet companies. They offered me a job at the end of the summer and asked me to start immediately and skip my second year at business school, but luckily David Thomas, always a guiding light, told me it was a bad idea. I was so excited because they wanted me and what I brought to the table, but like many young people in the entrepreneurial space, I didn't know what I didn't know. I was considering taking a job for equity with a company that was unproven. David knew better than I did that it was risky, and advised against it. I took his advice.

That was more than a lucky decision. In 1999–2000, the tech industry was booming. Alumni were returning to campus regaling current students with stories about sleeping in their cars while building start-ups, newly minted millionaires seeding the dreams of wannabe billionaires. Everyone wanted to start the next Pets.com and be a twenty-six-year-old CEO. It seemed like half of my classmates went to San Francisco for the summer between our first and second years. Tech drove booms in other industries too. It was also a crazy time for finance. The NASDAQ index, made up mainly of tech companies, hit what was then an all-time high in March 2000, but dropped by more than 50 percent by December.[1] Tech IPOs all but disappeared. The million-dollar signing bonuses, the promise of bottomless venture capital—all of it was gone. Suddenly there were far fewer job openings for business school graduates, which meant competition for offers was higher and compensation was lower.

Kia and I planned to finish our programs and move back to North Carolina, where I would go to work with Erskine at his private equity fund. Kia, who had been getting her master's in education at Harvard while I was at HBS, was going to teach. But then the universe threw us a beautiful curveball. One of Kia's professors encouraged her to apply for her doctorate, and she was accepted. We were going to be in Boston for a long time. That meant I had to find a job there.

I acted as if looking for a job was my job. I had an Excel

file where I made a list of everyone I had ever spoken to and when, with detailed notes and follow-ups—a book or an article they suggested or a contact I should reach out to. It wasn't an option to take the summer off after graduation to figure things out, as some of my classmates were doing. I had been awarded a scholarship through the Kraft Family Fellowship Fund (which would come full circle when Jonathan Kraft invested in WellWithAll), but I'd still graduate with debt. Growing up poor is like a double-edged sword when it comes to money. On the one hand, there's this constant, subconscious fear of being poor again. On the other hand, because I've been there, I know I'll do whatever it takes to provide for my family and myself. If I couldn't land a white-collar job, I'd have no problem becoming a manager at Lowe's. I wouldn't let myself suffer just because one path didn't work out.

I was interested in investment banking and private equity because of my relationship with Erskine. Plus, I knew that people like Erskine and Bob Rubin, the former treasury secretary, had built incredibly successful careers in investment banking before their time in politics. Erskine went into private equity after the White House. Many of my classmates were pursuing these paths, and they seemed like well-trodden roads that led to becoming a millionaire.

Erskine wrote about twenty letters of introduction to Boston finance firms on my behalf. Many of the companies felt an obligation to take a meeting with me, but no one offered me a job. Sometimes I wouldn't get a callback, or they would stall and say they were still working through their process. Others would say I wasn't "the right fit" but didn't give me any specifics.

Eventually, one of my Harvard Business School professors, Lynda Applegate, introduced me to Anne Margulies, an executive at a political consulting company. I almost didn't go to the interview because I had already worked at the White House and didn't want to go into politics, but I realized I should meet as many people as I could in Boston. I wasn't open to everything, but this was a reference from a credible source. It was an opportunity to learn something. Good people in your life can help extend your network. Plus, you never know where great opportunities will come from.

I approached the meeting with intellectual curiosity, researching the firm beforehand so I could show genuine interest and respect for what they were doing. I asked what had driven their success, and I made an effort to understand their journey. I wanted to make sure I did right by my professor's recommendation of me.

I talked to Anne for an hour. She asked about my time at the White House and Harvard Business School. I asked questions to get an understanding of their business. I told her about my interest in a career in finance. She got it and said, "You don't want to work here," but then introduced me to her boss, Tom O'Neill, son of Tip O'Neill, the famous Massachusetts congressman. That was an introduction I did not expect. Tom gave me the names of two people to call. Instead of seeing this as just a transactional moment, I approached it with an openness to learn and connect with someone new. I would've missed a once-in-a-lifetime opportunity if all I'd been thinking was, *What can this person do for me? Can they give me the exact job I want?* When you invest in gaining wisdom, in people, in community, good things happen.

One of the names Tom gave me was Phill Gross. Phill worked at Harvard Management Company, Harvard's non-profit subsidiary that managed the university's $18 billion endowment (now more than $50 billion).[2] The endowment is used to support student scholarships, investments in faculty, research of all kinds, and campus buildings and grounds. Phill was operating a hedge fund that was about to spin off into a stand-alone company, which they were going to call Adage Capital Management.

I didn't expect Phill to interview me for a job, but I was hoping he would introduce me to the person running the private equity division of Harvard Management Company. Tom O'Neill said that Phill was a brilliant guy, and I trusted Tom, so I was persistent and called Phill at least four times to try to get a meeting.

In preparation, I started an intense review of all the interviews I had done with private equity firms and technology companies while at HBS. I made a running list of all the questions I had ever been asked. I wanted to anticipate any perception of weakness around my inexperience in finance. I thought Phill might ask me "How will you make the transition?" or "Given that you haven't had a role in investing before, tell me why you're interested in this business?" I typed out responses, a script, not so I could respond robotically, but to ensure I had clarity of thought. I wanted to talk about watching my father build his tow truck company, which sparked my early interest in business. And I wanted to explain how my fascination grew at business school when I learned to identify and analyze well-run companies versus poorly run ones. At Harvard Business School, they teach using the case method: Every day in class we would discuss companies to learn about all aspects of business, from finance to marketing to operations. My classmates came from all around the world and from different industries, which meant we all benefited from their perspectives on being inside good and bad companies. I also learned that really great ideas can be poorly executed.

My knowledge of the investment world was limited, however. Google was in its infancy at the time, not really a helpful resource. Accounting is fundamental to understanding companies and how they work and generate profit, but it's a world away from the knowledge you need to invest millions of dollars into public or private companies. As an investor, you have to understand so much more—competition, market cycles, input costs and how they're changing, the dynamics of consumers, and the behavior that drives those dynamics. And on top of that, add the psychological volatility of investors' actions, which is constantly amplified by fear and greed in any given moment. Like any art or science, finance must be studied and practiced.

The fifth time I called Phill, he finally picked up and said, "I've been meaning to call you. What are you doing tomorrow?"

"Meeting with you?" I responded.

Phill and I met in his office in the Federal Reserve Bank Building in downtown Boston, overlooking the Fort Point Channel and the waterfront. We chatted about basketball, investing, and all kinds of subjects. At the end of our conversation, I asked him a question: "Based on what you know about me, is there anything that you think I should do or pursue?"

He thought for a moment. "What do you think about working for me?"

The truth? Just a few months before I didn't really know what a hedge fund was, but I didn't say that. While most of my classmates had specific goals during that time—*I want to work for a middle-market private equity fund based in Chicago that invests in infrastructure*—I had a much broader set of criteria. I wanted to work for someone who was highly successful and who wanted to teach me.

If you want to be an entrepreneur, you look for people who have grown multiple businesses. If you want to be an investor, you seek out someone with a long, proven track record. If you want to be a professor, you look for someone who is notably published. The point I'm making here is: Don't choose companies or high-level ideas—choose the people you want to learn from. That's how you'll gain the knowledge you desire, and that's how I've seen success happen.

I wanted to work for a person who had lived through cycles in an industry and came out on top. Success can be defined in different ways. Some say it's about money, but sometimes financial success is more about luck than skill, being in the right place at the right time, not something replicable. I wanted to learn from people who had a process, something that worked over and over again. And it was important to me that the person have respect for what I brought to the table. I wanted to increase my finance skills, to do more than accounting, whether that meant working for a serial entrepreneur in tech or the head of a financial firm, like Phill. Being open to opportunity and not myopic about what I thought I had to do to be successful was a key lesson for me.

Phill gave me an unpaid assignment, but the opportunity was so valuable to me that I would have gladly paid him to do it. The assignment was to analyze a blood pressure medication that was in phase 3 trials with the FDA and determine if it would be a good investment. I didn't know how to do that. I didn't know how to analyze the data. I didn't even know how to get the data. I had to call the company and ask them to send the data to me in the mail, not email, but via the U.S. Postal Service. Then I had to figure out what it meant. Then I had to imagine how the FDA would think about it and whether they would approve the drug. I needed a career's worth of knowledge in six months. Although I was still in school, I approached the project as if it were a full-time job, clocking late nights and early mornings. I borrowed statistics books. I spent hours poring over medical literature in the library. For months, Phill and I communicated through voicemail; he would leave me a message while I was in class and answer my questions, and I would respond with another message. Phill was trying to figure out if I was a self-starter or not, and whether I had the ability to climb the wall of knowledge that was needed. He wanted to know if I was honest enough to say "I don't understand" after doing a ton of work first.

I didn't understand a lot. I asked Phill about how the FDA made decisions and how stocks historically reacted to those decisions. Most of the time, what you'd think was a logical response to a company missing expectations or posting great results would turn out to be the opposite. There's a psychological game at play, in which people are constantly anticipating what others are anticipating. Often, the short-term reaction—what happens immediately after quarterly or annual earnings results—is completely different from the long-term potential.

Phill would talk to me about long-term investing and how to block out the noise. He emphasized that when markets are moving wildly and you're making or losing money every day, your own psychology becomes just as important as your analysis. Phill reinforced something I had learned at the White House: You can't get too excited or too down. You have to stay balanced emotionally to make good decisions in the midst of chaos.

Months and months went by, and while I was trying to understand the statistical analysis of the study, my classmates were getting offers from companies like Goldman Sachs and Bain & Company. But I wasn't envious. Only a few of my classmates went to hedge funds—most were focused on other sectors. For me, though, it wasn't about the industry; it was about the person. I had found exactly who I wanted to work for, exactly who I thought I would learn the most from. I put all my eggs in this one basket. *This is what I want to do,* I thought. *This is who I want to work for*. I focused all my time, attention, and energy on this one project. Eventually, through my analysis, I reached a conclusion: The drug would get FDA approval, and it was a sound investment.

Over those six months, I felt like I was taking another really interesting class while setting the foundation for my career after business school and developing a tremendous rapport with Phill through our back-and-forth conversations and questions. For Phill, it was less about the conclusion and more about the process. Anyone can guess a correct answer once or twice, but if you get the process right, your batting average will be far better than fifty-fifty. That's how he thought, and that's what he was assessing in me. I felt really great about the process I went through, what I had learned, and my ability to be helpful to him.

A couple of weeks after graduation, while Adage was still being established, with no money raised, no hiring processes in place, no human resources person, Phill offered me a job anyway, working under him. I joined what became one of the most successful investment firms and hedge funds in the country. In twenty years, we went from zero to more than $40 billion in assets under management. When I became partner five years after I started, I was the youngest partner at the firm by a decade.

Phill taught me that if I wanted to be great, I couldn't just do what the average person does. It wasn't enough to read the research reports. I had to do my own analysis, talk to suppliers, visit the stores, see how products were performing, how consumers were responding, and what salespeople had to say. I needed to truly understand how the industry worked.

Phill is a financial savant, exceptionally attuned to the delicate machinations of financial markets and business. He has a nearly photographic memory and the processing speed of a Formula 1 car. When a company takes what seems like a small stumble, and most people see it as a "great buying opportunity," he has the wisdom to recognize it as "catching a falling knife"—understanding there's still tremendous danger and it's not the right time to buy. Conversely, I've seen him double, triple, and even quadruple down on companies the market had written off for dead. While others would panic, cut their losses, and walk away, he stayed. Reacting to noise—"The stock is down, so I'm selling; the stock is up, so I'm buying"—is not what great investors do. Clarity of process is key. There are only a few things that drive the value of a business. Focus on those few things instead of the noise, and you'll be able to make decisions that others can't. Over time, that patience and conviction led to astronomical returns.

Phill operates on a higher level. His work ethic is unlike that of anyone I've ever met. But what sets him apart is his intellectual curiosity, the ability to ask that extra question. Knowing the company and the industry, being thoroughly prepared, and having the ability to ask the right set of questions separates you from conventional analysts. I've seen him skillfully challenge someone who was dodging a straight answer, cutting through to the critical issues and simplifying them.

Early in my career, I was in a meeting and the woman sitting next to me was an investor who had known Phill professionally for years. After the meeting, she turned to me and asked what I thought of the company that had just presented. I hesitated and said, "You know, I'm not exactly sure yet." She looked at me and said, "Phill would know exactly what he thought about a company after an hour-long meeting." That comment stuck with me. From that moment on, I was determined to always know exactly what I thought. Working with someone extraordinary changed my standards for success. I pushed myself to prepare at a level that could measure up to Phill's high standard and my own.

One of the most important lessons I learned from Phill is the need to have someone in your life who challenges you to be your best self. In my first couple of years at Adage, he took the time to go through models with me in painstaking detail to teach me how to analyze a company from a financial perspective. I've trained many others in the exact same way Phill trained me, making sure they understood the principles behind how I think about investing and running a company.

Phill taught me an invaluable lesson: While many leaders hoard information in an attempt to keep power, sharing knowledge and investing time in the less experienced members of your team makes everyone better; ultimately, everyone wins as a result.

Later in my career, Phill taught me something even more important. After five consecutive years of successful stock picking, I made a terrible investment. Up until that point, I had never seen a recession. I got a little cocky. I had invested in a good company, Pacific Sunwear, but I missed the magnitude at which the overall infrastructure of the retail industry was collapsing in 2008. Adage lost $20 million in a day and ultimately $50 million total on that investment. I had never experienced that kind of loss.

Phill wasn't angry; instead, he reinforced the idea that these moments had to happen if I was to become a great investor. He reminded me of my skills and capabilities and told me not to let this loss detract from the confidence I had in what I knew how to do. As I was trying to correct the mistake

I had made, I dug deeper into the industry. Most malls in the country were structurally broken. Amazon and off-price retailers like TJ Maxx, Ross Stores, and Burlington were steadily taking market share from mall-based retailers, and the valuations on both sides didn't even come close to reflecting that reality. The mall-based retailers were what I called "melting icebergs." I had found a significant investment theme that led to many, many multiples of gains as a result of that work.

Phill made more than a short-term investment in me. One mistake did not change that. As a leader and CEO, one thing I always tell my teams is that we need to be honest about the mistakes we make. This honesty builds trust in one another and in the truthfulness of our communication. We're human; we're going to make mistakes. The goal is to avoid making huge mistakes and to ensure we don't repeat the same ones. With strong preparation, hard work, and clear communication, we put ourselves in the best position to achieve this.

Sometimes we fall into the trap of thinking we know what the best candidate looks like, based on the school they attended or their class ranking or who they know in the world. When we measure achievement and success in what might seem like the most obvious and sensible ways, we run the risk of overlooking someone who could make a difference in our organization.

Mitch and Freada Kapor, venture capitalists and dear friends of mine, use a measure to evaluate candidates that I really love: distance traveled. Instead of looking at what someone has achieved, what elite positions they were able to attain, Freada and Mitch look at where a person started and how far they have progressed. Someone who has fought their way out of difficult circumstances can have grit, an internal motor, a level of desire to win that will be unmatched by any of the kids who breezed their way to Ivy League schools with SAT prep sessions and country club tennis lessons. The experience of having been in survival mode for so long means a person knows how to get a ton done. They have already done the improbable, so they aren't going to be afraid to stay up all night to find a solution or be broken down by one failure. Like me, these people have seen worse, and they are going to figure it out. It's worth taking another look at a résumé that doesn't seem like "the right fit" or answering an email from someone who had the courage to connect with you.

I have found that people who don't have social connections to diverse groups have a really difficult time with business connections as well. And it's not just about helping someone out; if you don't have diverse professional connections that are sustainable, then it's going to cost you money. There is an economic price to be paid for living in a homogeneous world. If you don't have a single person on your executive team who knows what Juneteenth is or who is paying attention to Hispanic Heritage Month, that's just one sign you're missing the breadth of knowledge needed to serve a growing diverse population in our country.

Firms scrambling after George Floyd's death lost money by not hiring (or fostering real relationships with) people like me long ago. The reality is that more than half of the young people in this country identify as a person of color. It's undeniable that our country has a clear (and moral) obligation to treat all groups with respect, though some try to deny it. Beyond that, the economic argument is crystal clear: Any company that chooses to ignore these groups over the next decade will suffer. Call it whatever you want, but serving these customers isn't just the right thing to do; it's good business sense. Over the past couple of years, we've seen a reversal of these efforts, but the economic implications remain the same. Black and Hispanic communities each represent more than $1 trillion in economic opportunity.[3] These are growing demographics, no matter how policies shift.

Phill is the single greatest investor I have ever met and, at the same time, one of the best humans I have ever known. He's a guy's guy, funny and affable and really into sports, an avid skier and a basketball fan. He is also incredibly optimistic and thoughtful. Like me, he grew up poor and despite his professional success is very down-to-earth. He has range: It's just as easy for him to be in a boardroom talking about the most complex scientific drug discovery process as it is for him to be in a dive bar eating chicken wings and drinking beer while talking about Jaylen Brown from the Celtics dunking on someone. Even when he became incredibly wealthy, he would still ride Peter Pan buses to his summer home.

Phill is deeply involved in philanthropy, generally in a very below-the-radar way, but in March of 2025 I was honored to present Phill with a leadership award he graciously accepted at a United Negro College Fund gala. Phill and his wife, Liz, provided $10 million through UNCF to Morehouse College and Howard University to kick off a program that equips students with essential skills and knowledge to prepare them for success in the financial sector. Like most of his investments, this will create wealth and lasting generational impacts.

The difference between Phill's actions and the uninformed responses I was getting in 2020 couldn't be starker. Phill is a friend of the good who was a catalyst for me, but his impact goes way beyond one person.

Chapter 8 Insights

- A true catalyst sees potential where others might see risk. Look for mentors who are willing to teach you and respect what you bring to the table.
- Preparation demonstrates commitment. When given a chance, treat it with the seriousness it deserves by doing the work others wouldn't.
- Measure candidates by "distance traveled" rather than just credentials. Someone who has fought their way out of difficult circumstances often brings unmatched grit and determination.
- Homogeneity has real economic costs. Organizations that lack diverse perspectives miss critical market insights.
- Stay open to unexpected paths rather than narrowly defining success. Sometimes the best opportunity comes from a direction you hadn't considered. You can learn a lot from a job or relationship you did not intend to pursue.

CHAPTER 9

Tara

Truth-Teller

Tara, a teaching assistant Kia befriended while working toward her doctorate, is a friend of the good who has shown me how to recognize reality exactly as it is—not as we wish it to be—while still maintaining hope and faith. When Tara was seven months pregnant, her husband died during routine surgery. Ten days later, her child was stillborn. The deaths of Tara's husband and child within two weeks of each other could have broken her, but they didn't. Instead, they moved her toward faith. She came through it with a strong sense that God was calling her to walk alongside others who are suffering. That experience gave her a kind of empathy, patience, and generosity that shows up in every part of her life—as a professor, a friend, and a mom. That experience also helped her learn to tell the truth, even when it's hard. In my life, Tara has shown me when I need to step up, how to be honest instead of endlessly optimistic,

> and that life can hold tragedy and joy at the same time and it's okay to feel both. Her capacity to acknowledge life's difficulties without being defined by them transformed how I approach challenges and relationships in my own life.

Right after graduation from business school, in June 2001, I started working at Adage Capital. I felt like I was back in those early days at the White House—there was so much to learn. I saw Phill's investment prowess and knew that to keep up I would have to drink from a fire hose. I didn't know anything about public markets or about being an investor. Not only was I investing in consumer companies, Phill's second love, but I was also analyzing healthcare companies. Many of the investors in healthcare are or were medical doctors or had significant medical training. And if you didn't demonstrate a level of competency and knowledge, those investors would judge you. I needed to understand and commit to memory terms that I'd never heard of, like *idiopathic pulmonary fibrosis*. I was trying to understand the impact of cardiovascular drugs, the complexity of the human genome, and new arthritis and cancer drug discoveries. Almost all of these drugs failed, but the rare successful ones were gigantic home runs. The volume of analysis in the healthcare world is mind-numbing.

Some say it takes ten thousand hours to master a craft, which equals about five and a half years if you work eight hours a day. I didn't want it to take that long, so I adopted the same discipline at Adage that I had learned at the White House. The office was usually empty when I arrived, and empty when I left at night. Sometimes Phill called my office line late at night to leave me a message and would be surprised when I'd pick up, still at my desk. I worked almost every weekend to get organized and prepared for the week ahead. Sometimes I'd spend twelve hours at the office on a Saturday. I didn't take a vacation that was more than a long weekend for five years.

Meanwhile, Kia was a doctoral student at Harvard. The program was incredibly competitive, a pressure cooker, and Kia was stressed from the workload. I was rarely at home. I wasn't there to give Kia any support or attention. I wasn't around for dinner or breakfast, and at night I would just pass out. She couldn't vent her own frustrations or fears with me. All I could think about was giving Adage Capital everything I had and getting ahead, getting us to financial stability—that was what I thought I was supposed to be doing. My idea of being a good husband and provider had come from my dad, who worked long hours, answering the call for his services whenever they were needed. If there was an accident at 3 A.M. and someone needed a tow, he was there. He did not have financial success, but he gave me the gift of a strong work ethic.

Kia's doctoral focus was on language and literacy, but she needed to pass statistics, which was a required course. I noticed she was working very hard, spending a lot of time with her tutor, Tara. Seeing her struggle, I did what I was used to doing, identifying the problem and trying to fix it. So I went out and bought a bunch of VHS tapes on statistics and regression analysis, thinking that Kia just needed a little boost. Of course, that wasn't the issue. Kia was working to her limits and so was I, but I was always putting on a brave face. I wanted to give the impression that we were handling it, we were just fine.

One day, when Tara was visiting, she asked me how I was doing and I said "fine," but Tara being Tara, she pushed further. "No, Demond, how are you *really* doing?" She told me what I was not seeing clearly: "You can't just fix this with a VHS tape." Kia didn't need me as a tutor; she needed me to be home, to listen, to not just be focused on my own stress. I had grown up in a culture where you kept going, where you handled things privately and didn't show cracks. So I focused on problem-solving instead of presence. Tara showed me that my brave face was actually a false face.

Tara and I both know how to project confidence and shape a narrative. We are both inclined toward positivity and perseverance. How I grew up, being vulnerable would get you killed or beat up or made fun of. Every instinct in me is to protect those I love and myself. I never tried to pretend that we were the perfect couple or some social elite. The way I grew up, problems were none of other people's business. I didn't understand that when you hide your problems from everyone, including those who love you, it becomes a kind of dishonesty, and you close yourself off from help and growth. That is where Tara's truth-telling changed how I operated.

She told me that when her husband and daughter died, the illusion that we can control things by working hard and staying positive died with them. All of her positivity, her work to find the right doctors, spending money to pay for care, knowing the right people, none of it changed the outcome. That devastation, she told me, set her free to understand that you can only control what you can control and leave the rest to God. This clarity made her a truth-teller.

And tell it she does—to herself and others. If she's too tired to help, she says so. If you're struggling, she checks in. If she and her second husband, Jeff, need to head back into therapy, she admits it. And if you are spending every minute at work when your wife needs you at home, if you're telling the world that your family is crushing it when they are in deep pain, she'll let you know. Through her honesty, she's created space for others to be real too. That's the kind of honesty she was inviting me into when she asked how I was really doing.

Over the course of our friendship, I have learned to answer Tara's question "How are you really doing?" with much more honesty and vulnerability. In a world that encourages us to present only our polished, successful selves, Tara's greatest gift has been showing Kia and me the power and freedom that come from embracing the whole truth of who we are. When all we share are our wins—our kids' achievements, our promotions, our curated vacation photos—we lose the possibility of a full friendship. There is no way to form deep and true friendships when we hide our truth—it only prolongs our pain. Tara's truth-telling isn't judgmental; it's liberating. She doesn't offer answers; she offers presence. When I started WellWithAll, I could tell Tara that I was scared. When parenting felt impossible, I could say it out loud. And I could cry. In the past, I would have held it together at all costs. Tara helped me see that two realities can coexist: Things will ultimately be okay, *and* right now things might be a complete mess. This is the essence of her truth-telling: bringing our challenges into the light as an essential part of the healing process.

I've also learned over time that imposing my way of thinking on other people isn't helpful. Tara has helped me learn, as a husband and a parent, that it is invalidating to a person dealing with a struggle to make suggestions and launch into "Why don't you just . . ." or "Maybe if you tried this . . ." or "I think your problem is . . ." or bring home a pile of how-to VHS tapes on statistics, like I did to try to help Kia. I haven't fully conquered this tendency! It still pains me to hold back from giving unsolicited advice, and I still do it sometimes. However, my perspective has shifted, and the way I deliver advice now is more empathetic, patient, and measured. It doesn't come naturally, but experience and practice have been incredibly helpful.

I can't fix everything, but I can be there for people. Tara has three children, each of whom has their own gifts and struggles. One experienced early trauma, one struggled academically, and one struggled socially. Tara was heartbroken for them and often frightened about how the world might treat them. Tara shared those feelings with me. In the past, I might have been full of suggestions—*you should, you just need to . . .*—but I can't fix a mother's heartbreak. I learned to listen.

Kia and Tara talk daily, often about their husbands and families. They listen without piling on. When Kia is unfairly pissed off at me (it's rare that it's unfair), Tara is the best person to tell her. (Thank you, Tara!) That's a friend of the good, someone who helps you see your way through.

For more than a decade, Tara, Jeff, Kia, and I have worked

together in our church marriage ministry, helping couples be honest and open about their struggles and fears and anxieties. We've built a community around transparency, which has helped many marriages, including ours.

Tara's commitment to truth-telling extends far beyond our family. She and Jeff have opened their home to students, formerly incarcerated people, those in recovery, a young woman from church whose mom died, and families fleeing violence and persecution in Afghanistan. Many arrived traumatized, disoriented, and grieving. Tara doesn't pretend to have all the answers or the power to fix everything. This is part of her truth-telling. She acknowledges the hard reality of someone's situation and then shows up and offers what she can—nothing more, nothing less: *This is hard, and I can't fix it, but here is a bed. Here is a shower. Here's how to make coffee.* Tara believes that God pushes back the darkness one act of hospitality at a time and considers herself blessed to walk with people wherever they are in the darkness. In their presence, she sees the presence of God.

Almost every one of my closest friends has lived through extraordinary trauma, which has equipped them with extraordinary compassion. They don't look away. They show up. They know their presence matters more than their polish. They can sit in the truth of what is happening and not run away. They ask questions. They step forward. They reach their hands out and show up. They show up at birthdays, go to school plays, and attend weddings. They show up when you come in last place, when your spouse leaves, and when you're sick and not getting better. They keep showing up.

Tara and Kia do that for each other, and they have taught

their husbands to do it as well. We are aunties and uncles to each other's children, and at least one of us will be there to put the other three in the ground. That's because we are honest about the hard things, about our own limitations and failings. In that vulnerability, we experience our capacity to love and be loved.

I've had moments when work was absolutely incredible, with amazing successes, while things at home were in complete shambles. And I've had times when everyone at home was incredibly happy, but work was a total disaster. Both were true, and I've learned not to ignore either. Yes, I'm an optimist, but I've learned to stop pretending everything's fine when it's not, and to stop believing that struggle is something to hide. Joy and pain can coexist. Like Tara, I now believe that healing starts when we tell the truth—not just to others but to ourselves.

Chapter 9 Insights

- The most powerful form of truth-telling comes without judgment; it illuminates reality while preserving dignity and offering genuine support.
- Sometimes love means confronting what others aren't willing to see. Bringing pain into the light is essential to the healing process.
- Break the silence around struggles. Communities that treat pain as weakness create barriers to healing that truth-tellers help dismantle.
- True presence transcends problem-solving. Being with someone in their pain without trying to "fix"

them demonstrates a deeper form of respect and care.

- Being real encourages others to do the same. When you let go of the mask and show your true self, it encourages others to reciprocate and creates the conditions for true and meaningful friendship.

CHAPTER 10

Marriage Ministry

Community

My church's marriage ministry is a team of twelve people who organize an annual gathering for approximately forty couples to discuss one of the most important and challenging relationships in our lives: marriage. For fifteen years, Kia and I have dedicated ourselves to this ministry, initially thinking we were signing up simply to help others. What we discovered was something far more profound. The marriage ministry is a friend of the good that is a community, one that uses the wisdom of a collective, working together to strengthen marital bonds, reduce pain, and provide practical and emotional support. Through our involvement, we received unexpected gifts: better understanding of each other's needs, learning to say "I'm sorry" and resolve offenses, and clearly identifying what matters most to each other. Marriage is a commitment between two people, but it takes more than two to help a marriage flourish. Kia

> and I didn't fully understand what the day-to-day of a healthy marriage looked like, and we needed this community to work through some struggles. What a gift to have found ourselves among others who, despite our differences, shared the same values and have journeyed alongside us.

Dressed in a bathrobe, pajama pants, and a mullet-style wig, I climbed up the basement stairs with chocolate smeared across my face and a bag of Cheetos in my hand. I was the costar of an episode of "Waban Hills" with Kia. "Waban Hills," named after the neighborhood we lived in, was a series of skits Kia and I made for our marriage ministry's annual retreat. The skits illustrated, with humor, the conflicts couples face after years of marriage: money, communication, romance, and the divisions of labor and responsibilities. This particular episode was about how things change from year one in a marriage to year five and beyond. In the scene just prior to chocolate and Cheetos, I came up from the basement in a Captain America costume, muscles bulging, lifting weights, full of enthusiasm, and ready for action—a symbol of the energy we bring to each other when we first get married. We all go through phases when we take our spouse for granted. There have been times I've looked back at old pictures, seeing that I let myself go a bit, and thought, *What the heck was I thinking?* Once the babies come along and work gets crazy, you kind of stop worrying about your appearance because, hey, you have your mate. But really, I always want my wife to look at me and think, *Damn, that man is sexy!* I want to keep that spark alive, not just for me but for her too.

The marriage ministry was an old idea brought back to life in 2008 by our church pastor Bishop Brian Greene, to create a community focused on marriage, increasing the number of people tackling marital problems from two to many. He asked Tara and Jeff to lead it and find others to help. I remember when Kia asked me to come to a meeting at Jeff and Tara's house. I'm pretty sure Kia and Tara had already decided this was happening, but in my mind, I was way too busy to take on anything else. I had no idea then just how much of a positive impact it would end up having on our life and our marriage. Now, for more than fifteen years, Kia, Tara, Jeff, and I have served with Jen, Saul, Ore, Yemi, Isabelle, Jeffrey, Troy, and Elisa. The marriage ministry's goal is to examine the critical issues that couples face every day with honesty, vulnerability, and transparency. Some of us needed to learn or unlearn what we saw our parents do as we grew up. My dad was a provider. He worked constantly. I internalized the idea that being a provider is the way to show love, but that is not all my family needs. I am still working on the right balance.

A lot of the time, we have no idea how to reflect on life as we experience it. We go through hard times and joyous times without examining what happened and why. Even in a marriage, we can feel alone and frustrated, and don't always find the best ways through. Choosing the wrong path through a rough patch can destroy a marriage, when someone seeks solace or understanding elsewhere. The marriage ministry is a place of refuge for my marriage, and I know without a shadow of a doubt that everyone in this community loves me, supports me, and is rooting for me. I also know that, collectively, there is no problem pertaining to my life that we can't face together.

I don't think I was being superreflective about marriage before joining this community. I learned lessons from the books we read as a group, and the guest speakers' real-life trials and tribulations added so much perspective. On top of that, just being with the people around a table each month made me think about how to be a better husband, father, and human. Sometimes I would have no idea when an argument was over. I would move on while Kia had not. There were things she was still annoyed about that I didn't know needed to be resolved. These sorts of things build up like rust on a bike chain that eventually will no longer work—I didn't realize I needed some WD-40!

When you begin a romantic relationship, it is often sparked by attraction and fun. Maybe you meet someone with similar interests or a shared sense of humor. You take on adventures together, discover new things, learn from each other's stories. As you get more serious and think about marriage, you might dig deeper into your core values. Before marriage there is often some soul-searching and planning to consider how you might take on a lifetime as a couple. Some people do this through a religious institution, working with a priest, pastor, or rabbi. Some discuss it with parents or extended family. Some do it themselves, perhaps working through a list of questions. And some people do nothing at all. Kia and I talked a lot about marriage when we were dating. We discussed the importance of religion and Christian faith in our lives, something that mattered deeply to both of us. Even though she had spent more time in church growing up than I had, I always felt that God was charting my path. We talked about kids too. I was certain I wanted four; Kia wasn't as sure. From the start, we both knew we'd need to compromise and be flexible, but we loved each other so much that we were willing to do what mattered most to make each other happy.

Life is unpredictable, which makes marriage hard. The logistics of one person are fairly simple. Add another person and things get a little more complicated. Add one, two, three kids and you've got full-on organizational chaos: getting kids to school, getting to work, making dinner, doing dishes, doing laundry, paying bills, filing taxes, making travel plans. Not to mention the emotional labor of managing extended family relationships, dealing with the drama of middle school and high school, navigating office politics and regular politics and wondering, *Did anyone feed the dog? Fill the car with gas? Send Grandma flowers on her birthday?* Getting all of that done requires someone with the résumé of a chief operating officer. We don't often marry someone because we think they'll be a wiz at juggling schedules. Some of the things you loved about the person you decided to marry—their creativity, their ambition, their sense of adventure, their sexiness—might not seem as useful when the shit, literally or logistically, hits the fan.

Before we were married, I thought I was busy—Kia and I were both working all the time, and she was deep into her doctoral work while I was hustling to make partner. But once we added kids into the mix, life got a whole lot more complicated. Suddenly, we were juggling daycare logistics, two careers, meetings, and the chaos of emergencies, like someone getting sick or taking a spill on the playground. Sometimes I'd be stuck at an airport because of a canceled flight when I was supposed to be home with the kids, or Kia would have to cover a class because a colleague couldn't make it. Or right when the kids needed to be picked up, I'd have to meet with the CEO of Walmart. Who's supposed to change their schedule when an emergency happens? Is one person's work more important than the other's? The only way to handle all of this is with clear communication, love, and respect for each other.

It seems crazy that couples do all this alone, just two people. During wedding ceremonies, the officiant often says something like "Will you, family and friends, support this couple in their marriage, offering your love and encouragement as they embark on this journey together?" The people in attendance usually respond with a resounding "We will!" But the truth is, when the party's over, a lot of people disappear. We all hit the dance floor hard, eat cake, hug, and congratulate one another in our excitement for this new union, but then we all retreat into our lives. And as married couples we often become insular. We don't seek help when trouble comes our way; we hide the challenges we face and think that we need to deal with them in our own house, together, just the two of us.

If I were starting a business, I would recognize that there would be challenges ahead, both known and unknown, and I would assemble a team of people with a broad skill set, people of various ages and backgrounds, people who were aligned in a common purpose and who had similar values, people who were honest and supportive. That would allow me and my business to face challenges with the collective wisdom of the group, like the Avengers facing Thanos. In my personal life, that team is the marriage ministry.

One of the foundations of the marriage ministry is an annual retreat, which typically happens on Valentine's Day weekend. We head to a hotel, nothing glamorous, about thirty minutes outside of Boston—not too far away, but far enough for couples to get their kids out of their heads and focus on marriage for two days. Couples pay their own way, but if they cannot afford it, the church covers the cost. Any couple who wants to come is taken care of. It was important to Bishop Greene and the marriage ministry team that anyone who wanted to attend (and sometimes those who did not want to) could get the wisdom and connection from those retreats.

I didn't just see the people in the marriage ministry as folks who I went to church with who seemed nice and smart. I got to know them in a real way, and true friendships grew out of that. They became like family to me, people who I genuinely love and care about, who I want to check in on and help however I can. They truly mean the world to me. Of course, it helps that they're all good humans, but the work we do together lets me really see that. It pulled me out of the busyness of my own life and made me pay attention to the incredible people right in front of me. Without that work, I honestly don't think those deep connections would have ever happened.

Part of what bonds the group together is not just the retreat but the planning and building of this complex event. It takes a year, and it takes everyone. The marriage ministry gets together once a month in person or on calls to decide on topics, find a location, secure materials and speakers, and plan talks and activities.

Sometimes we choose a book we will read before getting together. We've read *Sacred Marriage* by Gary Thomas, which explores how marriage can deepen your relationship with God, and *The Five Love Languages* by Gary Chapman, a guide to understanding and expressing love in ways that resonate with your partner. In *Sacred Marriage,* I learned that oftentimes there are unresolved issues, like missing the kids' doctor appointments or being late to dinner on a Tuesday; the author referred to them as "open windows." If those windows aren't closed through apology or discussion, one spouse can't focus on what the other might want, like sex. So I started paying close attention and made it a point to close those windows every chance I got!

The agenda for our retreats included a variety of sessions led by different couples. The learning that happens when you are teaching something is immense because when you learn something to teach it, you have to go through it. We've had sessions with catchy titles like "For the Love of Money," clearly about financial concerns, one of the biggest and most common stressors in a marriage. But we also cover sex, communication, and giving. After the lead couple presents a topic for the session, others open up about how they are experiencing the issue. The level of honesty, vulnerability, support, and love is astounding. When you've been married for a while, you can think that what you are feeling is unique, but there is great comfort in knowing you are not the only ones. I remember being at a retreat about twelve years ago when Kia and I had been bickering for a few weeks. I was frustrated and felt like Kia did not understand me. I was under a ton of pressure as a husband, as a dad, and at work. And then someone got up and began to speak about their marriage. They were saying the same thing. I instantaneously felt less alone. The problems seemed less insurmountable. After the group discussion, couples talk privately and directly during what we call knee-to-knee time, bringing the collective wisdom into a one-on-one conversation. After that discussion, when I spoke with Kia, I had a much greater appreciation for her concerns.

Our group is composed of a lot of diverse folks. Other than our common faith, we couldn't be more different. Included in our group are a tenured MIT professor, a lawyer, a doctor, a high school counselor, several Harvard PhDs, a worship and arts minister, and folks who have been involved in technology startups. We come from varied ethnic backgrounds and several countries, have disparate levels of education and income, have distinct family structures, and are of various ages.

It's so easy to just circle up with people who have similar backgrounds—there is a gravitational pull—but then you might miss out on a unique point of view or a perspective that will benefit your life. In the case of the marriage ministry, I have learned from others' perspectives on charitable giving, household finances, intimacy, and parenting. Those shared thoughts and ideas helped us look at our challenges differently.

One of the sessions I led at a retreat about seven years ago was in response to the question "How do you deal with relatives who feel like they're entitled to the fruits of your labor?"

It is a question not everyone is asked and not everyone has to answer, but many do.

I told the group that one of the greatest disciplines you can develop is the ability to say no. This is especially true for first-generation folks who are taking that step beyond poverty, an emotional complexity that many of us have had to navigate. There's always this fear that you could end up back in the projects or back in a trailer. For me, the worst thing in the world would be not being able to provide for my family. When I shared my fears in the session, there was a lot of nodding and a lot of discussion. I let everyone know how we approached the situation by doing some things to help our family in ways that felt appropriate and respected what we could realistically handle. If we don't take care of ourselves and protect our needs, we can't help anyone else. So, yes, help where you can. Share what you know. Don't feel guilty about prioritizing your own well-being because if you're not okay, none of it works. There's a reason flight attendants tell you to put your oxygen mask on first.

That's one example of how the ministry shares knowledge that can help support a marriage because problems don't exist only between two people. Sometimes what members of our group need is more intimate and personal. At the end of one planning meeting, we had a prayer request. One couple who had gone through a series of miscarriages was pregnant again, and the pregnancy had been rocky and showing signs of distress. The baby appeared to be doing well, but the mother was spotting and basically on bed rest (but came to the meeting). The husband had to be away from home a lot because of work, and everyone was feeling stressed.

The husband talked about how he came from a culture that didn't discuss hard times with others. It had been ingrained in him *not* to share, and so even though they had been under such distress for months, he didn't want to mention it. He then got very vulnerable and talked about how the house was a wreck and how some support they usually had from a family member wasn't happening because of a health issue.

Hearing the couple be open about this experience and on the verge of tears impacted all of us standing in that prayer circle. I said, "What I'm hearing is you need more than prayer." Immediately the group began to organize meal delivery, a biweekly cleaning service, and people who could help directly began coming over to do so. And then we prayed; we asked God to give them strength and to protect the baby. Several months later, the baby was born, beautiful and healthy.

We've sat with one another in hospital waiting rooms while someone battled a life-threatening illness. We feed one another. We've housed whole families when someone was sick and needed help to move around or needed kids out of the house. There is a bonding effect from planning the retreat, but the support goes beyond those planning sessions and beyond those weekends. We share the tragedies and joys of life.

For more than fifteen years, Kia and I have known everyone in the ministry, and they have known us. They know every trial and tribulation, from my torn Achilles tendon to parenting disagreements to stress and pressure at work. There is no posturing. There have been times when I didn't know what was bothering me until I started talking to the group.

Figuring out what was breaking my heart, having people putting their hands on us, praying for us, we knew we were going to be okay.

When I made my failed investment in Pacific Sunwear, I lost a ton of money for the first time in my career. There was never any real doubt about having a job or opportunity, but it was still incredibly stressful—I had never been in that position before. I was embarrassed to lose the firm money after so many years of success. This was at the same time the stock market crashed in 2008. Other people were just as anxious, worrying about what was going to happen to the economy or if they might lose their jobs. Those were hard times for everyone. We all prayed together.

The marriage ministry believes that marriage doesn't have to be perfect. Imperfection doesn't disqualify you. We believe in marriage regardless, as a bedrock blessing. The time together, the work together, and the vulnerability of these retreats knits us together. We ask challenging questions. We also laugh a lot, mixing the deep with the absurd. On the last night of the retreat, we have a big party with a DJ, and the next morning we end with communion and prayer.

We are blessed to have the marriage ministry, but community as a friend of the good doesn't have to come from a church. Faith gives us a common core value, but that's not the only reason why the marriage ministry works. It works because we build something together—the retreat—and we have a group that is diverse, honest, vulnerable, loving, transparent, and has committed to one another over time. The community changes from year to year as people join and some move away or come back, but it's about a sustained connection and effort. The people who make up the group don't have to be your best friends—it's not really a one-on-one thing—but as part of this or any community, our shared purpose is what bonds us.

Chapter 10 Insights

- Marriage isn't meant to be navigated alone. Surround yourself with a community that can offer collective wisdom and support when challenges arise.
- Vulnerability creates connection. A willingness to be honest about your struggles reveals you're not alone, and problems can seem less insurmountable.
- All communities thrive on diversity. Seeking perspectives from people with different backgrounds, experiences, and viewpoints expands your understanding of both problems and solutions.
- Community is more than cookouts and birthday parties. It's about providing practical support during difficult times, from meals to childcare to simply showing up.
- Building something together creates lasting bonds. When you collaborate on a shared purpose over time, you develop trust and connection that mere socializing cannot create.
- Balance depth with celebration. The strongest communities can hold serious discussions about life's challenges alongside moments of joy, laughter, and letting loose.

AFTERWORD

WellWithAll

Coming Together, Full Circle

Unlike the chapters in this book, this afterword isn't about a single friend or group—it's about what happens when the lessons, wisdom, triumphs, and failures shared with all my friends of the good come together to create something bigger. WellWithAll embodies the energy and unwavering support others have poured into me; it's a living tribute to their spirit, their sacrifices, and the values they've helped shape in me. I lived through a lot and paid a price for the hardships I faced, but I made it through because others believed in me when I didn't always believe in myself. Now I have reached a point in my life where I want to be that same kind of friend—not just to individuals, but to society. I had always tried to give back, to pay it forward in quiet ways, but starting WellWithAll was different. It was my decision to build a vehicle for giving, a platform rooted in the good I received so that it could ripple outward into the world.

"I'm in. Let's go."

It was 2020 and I had called friend of the good Carmichael Roberts to ask if he would start a company with me. His response was immediate and without hesitation.

I first met Carmichael when he was an undergrad at Duke with my cousin Mo, but we became friends when we both settled in the Boston area. Carmichael had earned a PhD in chemistry from Duke and an MBA from MIT and established himself in the Boston business community as a venture capitalist. After he had founded dozens of companies, he oversaw investments in more than one hundred others. I made a habit of hosting dinners to bring together young Black men from Harvard Business School to talk about jobs, life, dating—all the things young men struggle with and don't talk about much. Carmichael was often there to lend his own quiet advice.

Early in our friendship, he sought advice from me about starting his own firm. We'd grab lunch every once in a while. Eventually we started discussing more personal things. Two of his family members were struggling with anxiety and depression. I told him about what my family member was going through. We talked about life as it came, the good and the bad, and over time we became closer.

Our lives have a tremendous number of overlaps. We had similar challenges in childhood. He moved from family member to family member in different homes and in rough parts of New York. We have both been married for decades and have children we love dearly. He has taken on the care of his extended family the way I do. We can go for a walk, and I can say, *This is what is happening with my kid/parent/wife/work, etc.,* and he'll say, *I understand,* because he does. The result is deep and profound trust. Our bond is not just nice or helpful; it means we can do amazing things together, like building a world-changing business.

When the Covid-19 pandemic hit, one of my family members withdrew into a deep depression. As we struggled with treatments, progress, and backslides, there came a day when we had to go to the hospital—an outpatient program would not be enough. We went to the ER and then we waited.

In my family and in my community, we never talked about mental illness. When my cousin Mo was growing up, he had an uncle whom everyone called "Crazy" Tim. During those summers in North Carolina, Mo and I would be playing hoops and Tim would roll up on his bike. Tim biked everywhere, sometimes wrapped in a parka on top of multiple layers of clothes, even in summer. He often wore a big backpack stuffed with a stack of papers. Tim insisted that he had won the Publishers Clearing House Sweepstakes and carried around an oversize check that he would present as evidence.

To me, Tim was just a local eccentric. He was, I now recognize, one of the first people in my life who had a mental health condition, but back then everyone just considered him odd and funny. In retrospect, I've seen a lot of depression and anxiety in people close to me—family, friends, and colleagues—but I didn't have the experience to recognize it, and it doesn't always look the same. Surrounded by family like Mo and neighbors who looked out for him, Tim was all right. But in a different environment, in a city or a place where he didn't know anyone, his circumstances could've looked very different. So many Black folks who have lived through hardship and trauma are dealing with true medical conditions, but they may not see it that way because the harm is not visible.

When my family member fell into depression, I thought about what our experience would have been like if I hadn't been successful in finance, and if our family hadn't built up wealth. What if this was me forty years ago, living in a bleak public housing complex in Inglewood, California, with a drug-addicted abusive stepdad and no health insurance? What if it was me when I was living in a trailer with my dad in rural North Carolina? I don't think I would have survived. Our family is incredibly blessed with prosperity and social capital, with powerful connections within the healthcare field. With these advantages, we are able to live healthier lives. Without them, the obstacles to our well-being would have been magnified a millionfold. And the reality is, that's where a hell of a lot of Black and Brown folks are today.

In our own backyard, Back Bay and Roxbury are two Boston neighborhoods that, while only three miles apart, have a difference in life expectancy of more than twenty years: ninety-two years of age in the predominantly white Back Bay versus sixty-nine in the predominantly Black and Hispanic Roxbury.[1] During Covid-19, we saw many of our friends, relatives, and members of our church pass away not because of the virus itself but because of underlying conditions that had gone unmanaged for years. They lacked adequate access to healthcare, and when the virus hit, it overwhelmed them.

At the core of these health disparities is a history of racism that was brought to the surface again around the same time we were dealing with the fallout from Covid-19 and our family member's mental health struggle. After the murder of George Floyd, colleagues, partners, and acquaintances would regularly call me to make sense of the world for them. *Why is this happening?* people asked me. *Why were you able to overcome obstacles to success while others were not? Is the world really as unequal and discriminatory as it seems? Was it always this bad, or has it gotten worse? What should we do about it?*

I was frustrated by the lack of knowledge and accountability of many people I knew. It's easy to ignore other people's experiences, especially when growing up in a bubble of private schools, elite colleges, and wealthy workspaces. Many folks believe opportunity is the result of their hard work and initiative, ignoring the advantages they have taken for granted. The presence of Black people in those bubbles convinces people that the system is now fair. We had a Black president after all. But that doesn't mean bias, discrimination, and racism are solved. People wondered how to change that. Part of me wanted to sit back and tell them, *You do the work; you figure it out.* It's not hard to see or understand if you just open your eyes to the world, but in addition to fielding phone calls I wrote an email to my partners at Adage, which I later sent to the entire firm and then a wider distribution of friends and colleagues on Wall Street. In it I talked about my experience with the police in Cambridge, about being mistaken for household staff at the funeral of a friend's family member, and about being the only African American partner at a financial institution like Adage in the country (which was a ridiculous but true statement).

I wrote that I held my position at Adage "not because I am the smartest Black person in the world. The leadership of Adage has been unique from the very beginning, not just for a firm in Boston, but unique in the freaking world. I write this to make sure that we keep that very special quality as leaders, colleagues and friends. As a start I suggest we make sure that when we interact with our African American members of the team this week we don't act as if what is happening is not happening. I suggest you say that things are not right, they need to get better AND individually we will do our part to make it better."

On another front in my work life, I was having a ton of conversations about how Black folks were being ignored by big consumer companies in the health and wellness space. In general, many people still considered products marketed to the Black population as "niche"—a niche totaling $1 trillion of spending power[2] and at least another trillion plus if you count people of Hispanic heritage.[3] PepsiCo was one of the first companies to hire Black executives to market to Black people as early as the 1940s, in recognition of that purchasing power,[4] but those ads and marketing campaigns were not considered for everyone. Consumer markets and marketing were still segregated. Through much of the twentieth century, if Black people were featured in an advertisement, those products were considered to be only for Black people. If white people were featured, then the product was for everyone. Coca-Cola did not feature Black individuals prominently in its ads until it ran campaigns like "It's the Real Thing" in 1969 and "I'd Like to Buy the World a Coke" in 1971, which included racially diverse consumers.

Putting it all together, I saw a ton of people who needed help, and I had a business idea that could drive a solution to that problem. As an investor, I figured I could find a way to serve those people and fill a massive hole in the consumer market. In 2021, the U.S. health and wellness market was valued at around $1.3 trillion, and it was growing.[5] People were generally more and more interested in living healthy lives, and the Covid-19 pandemic only increased that interest. The supplement market alone was worth more than $40 billion.[6] But Black consumers reported that health and wellness companies did not make an effort to reach them. Everything that had been going on in my life and in my head I had discussed along the way with Carmichael.

We decided we would focus on three areas: maternal, heart, and mental health. While health disparities exist across the board for Black and Brown people, the numbers in those three areas are particularly bleak. Black infants are more than two times more likely to die than white infants,[7] and "the [pregnancy-related mortality rate] for black women was 5.2 times that of their white counterparts."[8] Black people had a lower rate of being diagnosed with a heart attack or heart disease than their white counterparts but were more likely to die.[9] An American Psychiatric Association report showed that Black people had lower rates of receiving mental health services, and when they did, they were more likely to receive a poorer quality of care.[10] Between 2018 and 2022, deaths from suicide among Black adolescents increased and surpassed the rate of their white counterparts.[11]

This is where I wanted to focus. This is how I would double down on giving back. WellWithAll would be more than a business; it would be an extension of my life's work, a manifestation of the values instilled in me by my friends of the good. Miss Polly's foundational love and generosity would be at WellWithAll's heart and soul. The lessons Miss Johns taught me about using my strengths, understanding my weaknesses, and being willing to ask for help would allow me to build a company with confidence and humility. What I learned from Mo, to find a partner who shares your vision and doesn't limit what you think is possible, is fundamental to getting any entrepreneur's dream off the ground. My chosen family taught me about the power of community. And I needed truth-tellers, mentors, and my ride or die to give me feedback, correction with love, and have my back. I needed people I could trust and who trusted me.

So Carmichael and I got to work.

As an investor, I was deeply involved in the businesses I invested in, analyzing their operations, business models, and marketing, but that's not the same as starting something from scratch. There are so many decisions to make, from hiring and firing to dealing with the complexities of setting up legal and financial structures. You also need to raise money, which we had done at Adage, but only after we had a track record of positive returns. With a start-up, you have to convince people to invest, set up the structure, and ensure the legal documents are in place. These are things I'd never done before. Carmichael had that experience. He had been an entrepreneur multiple times, taking an idea from the brainstorming stage to commercialization. He also had the operational know-how I lacked.

Carmichael and I spent the next six months or so doing

research, talking to people, trying to figure out the market, developing the structure, and meeting with potential investors. Most people who explore an idea like this only talk to businesses that have been home runs. For me, it was critical to also learn from entrepreneurs who hadn't been as successful. We wanted to understand the pitfalls, or the potholes, we could avoid falling into. Often, this insight is even more valuable than understanding what success looks like.

Any successful business is built on a combination of grit, determination, and some luck. I was careful not to conflate luck with skill. I spoke to people who ran companies that grew too quickly, expanding faster than they could handle. Some had overordered inventory in an attempt to reduce costs per item, only to find themselves stuck with excess goods that created a massive drag on their cash flow. Others got overly excited when big-box retailers wanted them to go nationwide, placing their products in stores where no one had ever heard of their brand. These products didn't sell, and many of those same retailers eventually demanded to return the unsold inventory, creating huge financial problems. The vulnerability of the people who spoke to me was a gift, both their honesty about what went right and, even more important, mistakes that they made.

I considered starting a nonprofit organization, but I identified several problems in that space: everyone trying to raise the same dollars, donor egos getting in the way of on-the-ground expertise, a lack of collaboration, not to mention that Massachusetts has more nonprofits per capita than any other state. I am not denying that many of these organizations do a ton of good, but I didn't want to go out and beg for money every year. I looked at Patagonia's model, TOMS Shoes, and Newman's Own and analyzed their pluses and their problems. Paul Newman, through a for-profit company, has given away more than $600 million to help terminally ill kids and other causes.[12] Why couldn't I do the same thing, harnessing the potential of capitalism to positively impact healthcare, particularly mental illness, heart disease, and maternal health?

I wanted to produce high-quality products. We planned to launch a line of supplements carefully formulated and focused on the unique health challenges faced by our target consumer. Our products would be created and sold by people who legitimately knew the communities we aimed to serve. We wanted to connect with our communities directly instead of having our message trickle down from some marketing machine. And from the start, I wanted WellWithAll to be more than a company: I wanted it to be a movement. So we decided to direct 20 percent of our profits into health equity programs, with an ambitious goal of investing $300 million over ten years.

When we determined that the wellness industry was going to be our focus, I immediately called Michael Archbold, the former CEO of GNC and former president of the Vitamin Shoppe. I had invested in the Vitamin Shoppe when I worked at Adage and had known Mike for more than a decade. I convinced him to join as a founding executive in October 2021, which gave WellWithAll a major credibility boost. Carmichael and I shared our ideas with him, and he validated our thinking. Then he brought in an incredible group of people. Friends of the good reaching out to their friends of the good,

good people bringing in other good people. The team was coming together.

Initially, Carmichael and I planned to start the company and hire someone with managerial and start-up experience to lead it. I wasn't an entrepreneur, I had never started or run a company, but as we continued to talk, we began to realize that my brain worked like someone who had done those things. On a daily basis I believe anything is possible. This mindset was instilled in me during my time at the White House. There was never a moment when you told the White House chief of staff that something couldn't be done. You figured it out—got the right experts, made the calls, woke up earlier, and stayed up later. Erskine taught me how to be what he called a "doer," someone who gets things done. I could visualize the right partnerships, anticipate a plan B, and see opportunities that others might miss. I also had broad and deep personal relationships that I could use to help bring our concept to fruition, and I was personally invested in its mission. I wanted to do this, and so we decided I would become the CEO.

Carmichael and I talk a few times a week and text almost every day. We trust each other from a competency standpoint and a friendship standpoint, and that has become a powerful combination in our work together. He's brilliant, plus I know how his mind works. He adds value in almost every way, from coaching some of our executives to being a sounding board for new ideas and partnerships to advising on the legal structure and negotiations. His skills complement mine. The depth of my friendship with Carmichael means I never have to question his intentions as a business partner. We've made some big decisions together: how much money to raise, who to hire, what products to launch, who to let go. And while miscommunications happen, I never wonder if he has an ulterior motive. This saves a tremendous amount of energy.

When we set up our deal and figured out how to work together, we talked through our different roles in running the business. We wanted what was reasonable and fair. This isn't always the case in business deals. Oftentimes the reason people are trying to get the best deal they possibly can is because they're trying to mitigate risk. If you don't know the person, you don't know if they'll still be around a year from now, and you don't know if they'll follow through or actually do what they said they would. So people try to mitigate risk and put in safeguards to offset those risks.

For example, part of negotiating the price of a house is that you're trying to save money, but another part of it is, "Well, something could be going on in the basement that I don't know about and the water heater is going to blow and I'm going to have to spend an extra ten thousand dollars on it." Unidentified risk, the unknown, is what people are usually trying to account for in a negotiation.

When you have a twenty-five-year relationship built on trust, some of those risks are eradicated, but you do still need a contract or an agreement that maintains fairness, and the basic contract of ventures like these accounts for that with vesting. You don't get all of your ownership all at once in any enterprise; it happens over a four- or five-year period. As long as Carmichael and I do what we've said we're going to do, WellWithAll will economically benefit us in the way we intended. If I had chosen someone else to launch WellWithAll with, it would have taken years to build that kind of trust.

In addition to Carmichael's partnership, I needed a guiding light, so I asked Jim Cash to be a senior adviser to WellWithAll and help me figure out how to move from investor at Adage to CEO at WellWithAll. He made WellWithAll one of his highest priorities. While Jim believed my deep personal experience would help sustain me in my new role, he challenged me to think carefully about the transition because only a small percentage of people have done it successfully. He talked about the differences he saw between an investor's job (understanding a business's economic model) and an operator's need to understand culture and how to stay ahead of the competition. I viewed my new role and its requirements as a challenge rather than a barrier. By the end of 2021, with the support of Jim, Phill, and Kia, I made plans to leave Adage and pursue WellWithAll full-time starting in 2023.

The first person to invest was Ken Chenault, the former CEO of American Express, followed by Jeremy Sclar, CEO of WS Development, and David Fialkow, an award-winning film producer and co-founder of General Catalyst, who also gave me tremendous advice, made introductions, and even gave me office space. Other investors included Jonathan Kraft, president of the Kraft Group and the New England Patriots. Jonathan is the son of Robert Kraft, whom I met while I was a student at Harvard Business School and who was responsible for my scholarship. That memory was locked away in the back of my mind. Then, twenty years later, I became friends with Jonathan. It wasn't until I started receiving invitations to attend dinners for the new Kraft fellows that I realized how everything had come together. My mentors Erskine Bowles and Phill Gross also invested, and so did others I'd built relationships with or worked with over the years. Within a few months, we had raised more than $7 million. This collection of people knew me and my capabilities. They gave me wisdom, honest feedback, and encouragement. They reinforced the idea that the work we were doing was not just important—it was critical!

To fulfill our promise of giving back to the Black community, we needed to find the right partners to work with on healthcare and access in the three areas we had identified. Our first partnership was with the Dimock Center, a community health center in Boston's Roxbury neighborhood. When I walked into those apartment buildings, through the neighborhoods, past the bus stops, and into the doctor's office, I saw my own childhood. There were so many moments when I reached for the hands of grandmothers who thanked us for the work we were doing. I saw Miss Polly in each one of them. Every hour, every bit of work, gave me more clarity that this is exactly what I should be doing with my life, my time, and my skills.

In 2023, WellWithAll established the HEAL (Health Equity, Advocacy, and Leadership) Academy, a six-week program that trains Black, Brown, and underserved teens and young adults to serve as health ambassadors in their communities. While the HEAL Academy started in Boston, it offered a possible blueprint to expand the program to other cities. Every early partnership I engage in is with individuals who share common values and a commitment to doing good. These are people who run institutions with integrity and have a proven ability to execute. I had a long history of collaboration in various capacities with these partners. One was Dr. Charles Anderson, who runs Dimock, and is someone I have known for more than twenty years. A brilliant doctor, he has dedicated his life to serving those in need.

In 2024, to broaden our efforts to provide health information and care to those in underserved communities, I forged partnerships with Advocate Health, a nonprofit health system supporting six million patients across six states, UNCC, and the YMCA in Charlotte, which assists a community with the lowest life expectancy outcomes in the metro area.

Earlier, in 2022, Michael Archbold began building the foundation for our supplement line, applying his expertise to develop products backed by clinical research. The collection included formulations designed to help maintain healthy blood pressure, blood sugar, and cholesterol levels. We made sleep support a priority for communities of color because we wanted to challenge the "hustle harder" mentality while promoting rest, mental wellness, and recovery. We incorporated vitamin D, important for immune health, recognizing that deficiencies frequently occur in communities of color since the higher melanin content in darker skin reduces the body's ability to produce vitamin D when exposed to sunlight.

We also wanted to develop an energy drink. We brought in experts to tap into a health and wellness consumer base that had $1 trillion of spending power, but we needed help with manufacturing expertise and scale. We decided to partner with Campbell's. We drove the development using Campbell's resources, and I personally chose the direction of the first flavor. Nostalgia for fruit punch guided me, and as a team, we committed to making it an all-natural drink that had as much caffeine as a cup of coffee but was also vitamin fortified, naturally sweetened, low-calorie, and free of added sugar. The energy drink moved us into the fitness side, or what is called "active wellness." In partnership with Campbell's, we created a product in nine months that would have taken us five years on our own.

One thing we did that I felt was critically important was stepping away from the standard testing route most companies follow. Instead, we spent extra money and added an extra month to the development process to bring in consumer panels that represented Black, Hispanic, and Caribbean people, ensuring their voices were heard in shaping the product. We didn't just bring in who was easily available to do this work. This approach was almost unprecedented. Most companies wouldn't have gone as far as hiring an outside agency to specifically recruit a diverse group of people to taste-test the product and provide detailed feedback. After receiving that feedback, we made adjustments to ensure people would truly love the taste. Throughout the process, in the back of my mind was Indra Nooyi's message that they had to love the taste.

This approach comes from my background. Having spent more than twenty years reflecting on how seemingly unrelated factors could significantly influence the public companies I invested in, I've trained my mind to constantly extrapolate and connect dots. The experiences that shaped me—working at the White House, collaborating with Erskine, working for Phill, and overcoming the challenges of my childhood—have given me a unique perspective and drive.

You can see this in my daily rhythm. I start most mornings at five-thirty and typically go to bed around eleven. When I'm not spending time with family or friends, my mind is almost always focused on business or finding ways to help people more effectively. My team often sends me Running Man emojis because they're hustling to keep up with my pace.

I've had to learn to manage the volume and speed of my requests to avoid overwhelming those around me. Going too fast could be great, but it could also be our downfall. So we have worked on building a culture where people are comfortable challenging me; we don't want loyalty to get in the way of good decision-making. I've learned to present my vision more incrementally, acknowledging that while I may see the destination clearly, we may not be able to do everything immediately.

My pace is something I've come to realize is very different from most. Carmichael has been great at reminding me never to slow down to match someone else's pace because the innovation has to keep moving forward. I need people around me who can support and fuel that momentum. I'm getting better at filtering and helping people understand what's essential right now versus what can wait for the future.

A key part of engaging our target consumer included joining and creating conversations about their health and wellness journey, weaving together product, community, and purpose. I personally participated in several high-profile events around mental health, including the *Black Enterprise* Men XCEL Summit. On Martha's Vineyard, I spoke at the Disruption Dialogue Series and Boston Medical Center's Elevating Health Equity's DonVersation with Don Cheadle. So many people connected to the vision in a really powerful way. Every time I tell my personal story with real vulnerability and truth, in almost every room, someone says they are going through the exact same thing.

Everything kind of came together at ESSENCE Fest. You couldn't miss our branding anywhere, from arrival at the airport to hotel displays to event spaces. Our team organized various wellness sessions, including beachfront yoga and group walks along the waterfront. The enthusiastic response to both our brand identity and the beverage really validated what we were doing. We constantly fielded questions from people wanting to know where they could buy it. Witnessing firsthand how people immediately connected with the drink was incredible. This beverage creates an entirely new pathway for introducing our brand and engaging with customers in ways that supplements simply cannot match.

During the festival I was invited to speak as part of a panel about men's mental health in the Black community. The lineup was amazing: brilliant actors Anthony Mackie and Omar Dorsey, hip-hop legend D-Nice, and supertalented businessmen and health advocates who happen to be brothers, Kainon and Kendell Jasper. I know D-Nice well, and Kendell and I actually went to college together. He's somebody I've always just loved like a brother from day one. But I didn't know Omar Dorsey, Anthony Mackie, or Kendell's brother, Kainon.

Over the several days that we were there, we spent time together talking, laughing, and joking. Then, when the panel happened, it was pretty magical. It almost felt like the crowd wasn't even there because we just began to talk about brotherhood, mental health, the struggles we've all gone through, and the need for friendship. D-Nice talked about feeling isolated and alone during the pandemic and how Kainon drove across the country to be with him. I told the audience how important it is for men to have honest and open conversations with one another, allowing a place for them to be vulnerable, because suicide rates are rising, especially among Black men and teens. It's so important, even necessary, for men to have true friendships and bonds. When times of crisis come, you need to know exactly who you can depend on to help make it through the inevitable pain and suffering in life.

In that hour-long conversation, we formed a brotherhood. And as a result, we are now all on a group text. There's not a day that goes by without communication from this group—complete comedy, brilliant commentary on what's happening in the world, or extraordinary vulnerability when one of us is going through something. That panel, and that time together, helped us all see that we were already friends in the truest sense, creating a daily connection that enhances my life. More friends of the good.

When it came to naming this company, it was a collective process that reflected our deeper aspirations for what we hoped to accomplish. We wanted to create something that embodied the idea of "well with all"—not just wellness for individuals but a vision where the health of each person is connected to the well-being of others. My own life and the business model we've built are inseparable: Years of giving back, learning from mentors, and experiencing both successes and failures have shaped this journey. I couldn't have started this company a decade ago; it took years of personal growth, support from my community, and the wisdom gathered from others to be ready to do this work in a meaningful way.

Experiencing hardship and loss gave me a new perspective on what it means to make an impact. The love and support I received during those times, from friends, family, and mentors, helped me get to where I am today. Now, with WellWithAll, I see an opportunity to be a friend of the good to society, to use what I've learned and the resources I have to help others live healthier lives. This isn't just about giving back; it's about creating real, positive change through our products and our actions, and being all in on making a difference for every community we touch.

WellWithAll brings it all together, all of my life experiences and the power of what friends of the good bring. It is a testament to the idea that you don't have to do it alone; in fact, you shouldn't. WellWithAll is showing up and trying to solve a problem while listening to the community our work is intended to support. I truly believe that WellWithAll will continue to grow and thrive as a direct reflection of all these things, and I won't stop until it's truly well with all.

Afterword Insights

- Your personal pain can become your purpose. The challenges that break your heart may reveal the very problem you're uniquely positioned to solve.
- When you talk about the mistakes you've made or the things you don't fully understand and break down the illusion of perfection, it creates a culture of vulnerability and transparency. This openness helps

build stronger connections and trust within your team.

- Relationships built over decades, ones based on trust, create opportunities that money can't buy. Years of friendship provide the foundation for making difficult decisions without questioning each other's motives.
- Learn from failures, not just successes. Seek out entrepreneurs who were unsuccessful to understand pitfalls rather than studying only the winners.

NOTES

Foreword

1. Carolyn Bruckmann, "The Friendship Recession: The Lost Art of Connecting," Harvard Kennedy School, Center for Public Leadership, February 2025, https://www.happiness.hks.harvard.edu/february-2025-issue/the-friendship-recession-the-lost-art-of-connecting.
2. Daniel A. Cox, "The State of American Friendship: Change, Challenges, and Loss," Survey Center on American Life, June 8, 2021, https://www.americansurveycenter.org/research/the-state-of-american-friendship-change-challenges-and-loss/.
3. Office of the U.S. Surgeon General, *Our Epidemic of Loneliness and Isolation: The U.S. Surgeon General's Advisory on the Healing Effects of Social Connection and Community,* Department of Health and Human Services, May 2023, https://www.hhs.gov/sites/default/files/surgeon-general-social-connection-advisory.pdf.

Introduction: What Is a Friend of the Good?

1. Aristotle, *The Nicomachean Ethics*, trans. Harris Rackham (Wordsworth Editions, 1996), 209.

2. Aristotle, *The Nicomachean Ethics,* 227.
3. Office of the Surgeon General, *Our Epidemic of Loneliness: The U.S. Surgeon General's Advisory on the Healing Effects of Social Connection and Community,* Department of Health and Human Services, May 2023, https://www.hhs.gov/sites/default/files/surgeon-general-social-connection-advisory.pdf.
4. Julianne Holt-Lunstad, Timothy B. Smith, and J. Bradley Layton, "Social Relationships and Mortality Risk: A Meta-Analytic Review," *PLoS Medicine* 7, no. 7 (July 27, 2010), https://journals.plos.org/plosmedicine/article?id=10.1371/journal.pmed.1000316.
5. Claire Cain Miller, "Today's Teenagers: Anxious About Their Futures and Disillusioned by Politicians," *New York Times,* January 29, 2024, https://www.nytimes.com/2024/01/29/upshot/teens-politics-mental-health.html.
6. Richard Reeves and Will Secker, "Male Suicide: Patterns and Recent Trends," American Institute for Boys and Men, November 17, 2023 (updated September 2024), https://aibm.org/research/male-suicide/.

Chapter 1: Miss Polly

1. Sara M. Moorman and Jeffrey E. Stokes, "Solidarity in the Grandparent-Adult Grandchild Relationship and Trajectories of Depressive Symptoms," *Gerontologist* 56, no. 3 (2016): 408–20, https://pubmed.ncbi.nlm.nih.gov/24906517/.

Chapter 4: Nick, Earl, Kevin, and Alpha Phi Alpha

1. Franklin Hughes and David Pilgrim, "Alpha Phi Alpha and Civil Rights," Question of the Month, March 2019, Jim Crow Museum, Ferris State University, https://jimcrowmuseum.ferris.edu/question/2019/march.htm.
2. Flinders Centre for Ageing Studies, "The Australian Longitudinal Study of Ageing (ALSA)," Flinders University, accessed July 3, 2025, https://sites.flinders.edu.au/alsa/.
3. U.S. Census Bureau, "Census Bureau Releases New Educational

Attainment Data," press release, February 16, 2023, https://www.census.gov/newsroom/press-releases/2023/educational-attainment-data.html.

Chapter 7: David and Jim

1. Equal Justice Initiative, "Five Years After Ferguson, Policing Reform Is Abandoned," August 12, 2019 (accessed March 26, 2025), https://eji.org/news/five-years-after-ferguson-policing-reform-abandoned/.
2. Chris Metinko and Gené Teare, "Drop in Venture Funding to Black-Founded Startups Greatly Outpaces Market Decline," *Crunchbase News,* February 27, 2024, https://news.crunchbase.com/diversity/venture-funding-black-founded-startups-2023-data/.

Chapter 8: Phill

1. NASDAQ Composite Index (COMP), NASDAQ.com, https://www.nasdaq.com/market-activity/index/comp.
2. Harvard University, *Financial Report: Fiscal Year 2024,* October 2024, https://finance.harvard.edu/files/fad/files/fy24_harvard_financial_report.pdf.
3. J. Merritt Melancon, *UGA Today,* August 11, 2021, https://news.uga.edu/selig-multicultural-economy-report-2021/.

Afterword: WellWithAll

1. Massachusetts Healthy Aging Collaborative, "Boston Public Health Commission Report Highlights Disparities in Life Expectancy Between City Neighborhoods," May 18, 2023, https://mahealthyagingcollaborative.org/boston-public-health-commission-report-highlights-disparities-in-life-expectancy-between-city-neighborhoods/.
2. McKinsey Institute for Economic Mobility, "The State of Black

Consumers: An Opportunity for Growth and Equity," McKinsey & Company, April 25, 2023, https://www.mckinsey.com/institute-for-economic-mobility/our-insights/black-consumers-and-the-opportunity-for-growth-and-equity.

3. "The Power of the U.S. Hispanic Consumer," *Adweek,* https://www.adweek.com/sponsored/the-power-of-the-u-s-hispanic-consumer/.
4. "How Corporate America Came to Recognize Diversity, One Pepsi at a Time," *Knowledge at Wharton,* February 28, 2007, https://knowledge.wharton.upenn.edu/article/how-corporate-america-came-to-recognize-diversity-one-pepsi-at-a-time/.
5. Precedence Research, "U.S. Health and Wellness Market Size, Share, and Trends 2025 to 2034," updated July 7, 2025, https://www.precedenceresearch.com/us-health-and-wellness-market.
6. Shaun Callaghan, Martin Lösch, Anna Pione, and Warren Teichner, "Feeling Good: The Future of the $1.5 Trillion Wellness Market," McKinsey & Company, April 8, 2021, https://www.mckinsey.com/industries/consumer-packaged-goods/our-insights/feeling-good-the-future-of-the-1-5-trillion-wellness-market.
7. Centers for Disease Control and Prevention, Maternal and Infant Health, "Infant Mortality," September 16, 2024, https://www.cdc.gov/maternal-infant-health/infant-mortality/?CDC_AAref_Val=https://www.cdc.gov/reproductivehealth/maternalinfanthealth/infantmortality.htm.
8. Centers for Disease Control and Prevention, "Racial and Ethnic Disparities Continue in Pregnancy-Related Deaths," CDC Archive, September 5, 2019, https://archive.cdc.gov/www_cdc_gov/media/releases/2019/p0905-racial-ethnic-disparities-pregnancy-deaths.html.
9. Nambi Ndugga, Latoya Hill, and Samantha Artiga, "Key Data on Health and Health Care by Race and Ethnicity," *KFF,* June 11, 2024, https://www.kff.org/key-data-on-health-and-health-care-by-race-and-ethnicity/.
10. American Psychiatric Association, "Mental Health Disparities: African Americans," 2017, https://www.psychiatry.org/getmedia/bc6ae47f-b0aa-4418-b045-952ede06757f/Mental-Health-Facts-for-African-Americans.pdf.
11. Farzana Akkas and Allison Corr, "Black Adolescent Suicide Rate

Reveals Urgent Need to Address Mental Health Care Barriers," Pew, April 22, 2024, https://www.pewtrusts.org/en/research-and-analysis/articles/2024/04/22/black-adolescent-suicide-rate-reveals-urgent-need-to-address-mental-health-care-barriers.

12. Newman's Own, "The Mission," https://newmansown.com/mission/.

ACKNOWLEDGMENTS

There is no such thing as a self-made man. If *Friends of the Good* stands as a testament to anything, it is to the extraordinary community of people whose love, wisdom, presence, and grace have shaped my life. Every chapter of this book is a reflection of the people I name here—my friends of the good—who have carried me forward, walked beside me, and called me higher.

To the many friends, family, and mentors who have poured into my life—whether in word, presence, prayer, or partnership—thank you. You are in these pages even if your name isn't.

To Corey Hajim, who brought twenty-five years of friendship, clarity, and soul to this book—your belief made the difference. You helped me find the structure and spirit needed to make this story whole, and I am forever grateful.

To Michele Norris, thank you for your brilliance, heart,

and steady guidance throughout this journey. Your insight shaped the very DNA of this project.

To Michelle Obama, thank you for your support, your example, and your enduring grace.

To my agent, Gail Ross, thank you for your wisdom, advocacy, and belief in this book before it had a single page.

To Jennifer Baker, our editor, thank you for your belief in this book, your thoughtful guidance, and your editorial brilliance. And to the entire team at Storehouse Voices and Penguin Random House—thank you for helping this story find its way into the world with care and purpose.

To every friend of the good—thank you. Your love is the thread that runs through this book and my life. I carry you with me, always.

With deep gratitude,
Demond Martin

"What role would you like to play in this book process?"

That was the text I received from Demond one evening in March 2024. After reading the book proposal (HUGE shoutout to Theo Emery for that foundational work), I couldn't stop thinking about Demond's personal story, life lessons, and deep insights about friendship. It was exactly the kind of project I wanted to take on. Though I wasn't certain what he was asking me, I wrote back, "My first, from the heart answer is, I'd like to write it." Demond responded immediately that he was thinking the same thing, and we planned to speak the following weekend. And so began our adventure together.

Demond is a friend of the good who is a kindred spirit.

We met in business school in 1999. It might not seem like we have much in common, but like so many FOTGs, what we share runs deep—our commitment and love for family, friends, laughter, and trying to do good things. Over the years those values have kept us coming back together.

Thank you, Demond, for inviting me to write this book with you. It has been an experience full of growth and joy—more joy than anyone should expect in such a big undertaking. Thank you for trusting me. And thank you for taking me to Bill's back in the day, reminding me to get away with my husband for romantic weekends, passing along great parenting advice, pumping me up when I need a boost, and always encouraging me to see the good in myself. I am so grateful.

Thank you to my lifelong friends of the good: Dane, Gina, Meaghan, and Glenn; my chosen families from TED (coworkers, speakers, and community) and HBS; Anne Morriss and Frances Frei; the Miller-Seo, Baillie, and Osman families; and many more—I cherish you.

I also want to thank a few people who taught me how to write: Bob Safian, Andy Serwer, Helen Walters, and Dylan Marron. And now, Jennifer Baker! Our brilliant editor from Storehouse Voices—thank you, Jenn, for pushing us (again and again) to the next level. Your patience, partnership, and expertise made a tremendous difference.

And finally, to my husband, Jim, who puts up with my bouts of self-doubt and pain-in-the-assery and never makes me feel bad about it, who always helps me find the funny, and who is very hot ;-), and not just for his age. To my kids, Lilith, Sammy, and Oscar, who fill my life with love and laughter and remind me I have a lot to learn. To my brother, Brad, who always has my back, and Marthe, GB, Karen, Ann, and extended family. And to my parents, Ed and Barbara, who have given me foundational love along with so many of the other good things mentioned in this book. Thank you.

—Corey Hajim

ABOUT THE AUTHORS

Investor and philanthropist Demond Martin is the cofounder and CEO of WellWithAll, an innovative health and wellness company that pours a significant portion of its profits into health equity for Black, Brown, and underserved communities. Prior to becoming CEO of WellWithAll, Demond was a senior partner at Adage Capital Management where he invested in the consumer sector for twenty-two years. Demond and his wife, Kia, focus on erasing gaps created by racial and social injustice in the areas of education and healthcare through philanthropic programs such as The Martin Scholars.

Corey Hajim is a writer and story editor who has spent most of her career (the fun part) helping people share their most powerful ideas. During her time as the business curator for TED Conferences, she worked with hundreds of influential thinkers—from Fortune 500 CEOs to groundbreaking entrepreneurs, authors, and academics—to craft talks that have reached millions globally. A former *Fortune* magazine reporter and equities investor, Hajim holds an MBA from Harvard Business School and a BA from the University of Vermont.

ABOUT STOREHOUSE VOICES

Storehouse Voices celebrates culturally rich narratives that reflect the dynamic influence of communities across the globe. Our imprint is dedicated to amplifying underrepresented and overworthy voices in fiction and nonfiction, with a focus on accessible and engaging content that honors the past, disrupts the present, and imagines new futures.

Learn more about us at storehousevoices.com.